Grimes Mill

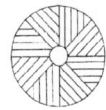  

Kentucky Landmark on Boone Creek, Fayette County

Harry G. Enoch

HERITAGE BOOKS, INC.

Other Heritage Books by the author:

Affair At Captina Creek

In Search of Morgan's Station and "The Last Indian Raid in Kentucky"

Published 2002 by
HERITAGE BOOKS, INC.
1540E Pointer Ridge Place, Bowie, Maryland 20716
1-800-398-7709
www.heritagebooks.com

ISBN 0-7884-2031-3

To
Jennifer and Jamie

Contents

Illustrations

Preface

Grimes Mill Road, a popular country drive in the Bluegrass, passes through the scenic Boone Creek gorge, beautiful in fall, in spring, or any season you happen to visit. Near the end of a steep grade, as you approach the creek from the west, the narrow road makes a sharp left turn. There in the curve, just off the right side of the road, stands an impressive stone edifice—Grimes Mill—a relic from Kentucky's past, unadorned by sign or marker. Soaring cliffs on the east bank tower over the mill, ascending more than a hundred feet above creek level.

Grimes Mill was one of the state's early water-powered gristmills, only a few of which remain standing. This two-and-a-half-story stone structure, thirteen miles southeast of Lexington, was built in about 1807 for Charles Grimes. The gristmill operated for over a century, prospering for about half of those years and then holding out against steadily worsening economic conditions until 1928, when the property was sold to the Iroquois Hunt Club. While the club has used the building now for over seventy years, they have conscientiously conserved the original materials and character. The Grimes Mill complex and the nearby Grimes House are listed on the National Register of Historic Places. The mill and house, both constructed from local limestone and beautifully preserved, are valuable examples of early Kentucky stone architecture.

The mill itself is probably more visible and illustrious today than ever before. Being home to the Iroquois Hunt Club, it is the place where hunters, horses, and hounds converge each fall for colorful foxhunts. These affairs are faithfully covered by local writers and photographers. The background for these events and the star of the show, of course, is the stately old mill.

Gristmills were among the first industries of early Kentucky and one of the most important. Corn was the chief crop of newly settled farmers. It was easy to plant, cultivate, and harvest, yielded a high output per acre, and could be stored for a long period. It was a staple of the pioneer diet, made a quality feed supplement for livestock, and could be converted to whiskey, a product with a ready

vii

market. One drawback was the fact that converting corn to meal using hand-powered mills was a time-consuming, labor-intensive process.[1] The gristmill substituted water power for human power. Flowing or falling water was applied to turn a strategically-placed paddle wheel, which then turned a set of axles and gears that ultimately turned the millstone. A pair of millstones often represented the major investment for a mill. The best ones, "French buhrs," had to be imported. The bottom or bed stone remained stationary. The top or runner stone, positioned less than an inch above the bed stone, rotated, and corn or wheat (the grist) was ground in the space between.[2]

Since they provided a nearly essential service for the farmer, gristmills were recognized as a public utility. Their importance is indicated by the fact that counties were given the power of imminent domain to secure land for mill sites, and at one time millers were excused from military duty. A sizeable body of law regulated the miller's practice. Mills sprang up by the hundreds before 1800 and later grew to several thousand. They appeared on every stream with sufficient water to turn a wheel and drive a pair of millstones. Some of the mills were crude log affairs that had a short life span, while others were substantial works that operated for many decades. In its most common form, these businesses served farmers who could conveniently reach the mill by wagon or on horseback, have their corn ground, and return home the same day. These were "custom mills" that ground corn in return for a share, usually an eighth, of the meal. The miller's share, his toll, was set by law. There were also "merchant mills" that produced flour and meal for sale rather than for the farmer. While the grinding process was essentially the same, the business model was distinctly different. The merchant mill purchased grain, usually in larger quantities than custom mills, and the product was packed in barrels for shipment to market. Of course, nothing prevented a merchant mill from also doing a certain amount of custom grinding.

Whether custom or merchant, these early manufacturers were closely tied to the agrarian economy, and most would not survive the transition to the modern industrial age. After the mid-nineteenth century, water-powered gristmills continued to function profitably in remote rural areas, but the more efficient roller mills began to dominate in urban centers. Gristmills near cities the size of

Lexington had to adapt and find new ways to generate revenue. Grinding corn, rye, and barley for distilleries was one niche that allowed mills to continue for a time. The demise of water power continued, however. The number of mills declined steadily throughout the twentieth century, and today only three operating mills remain in Kentucky.

Grimes Mill was born during the mill-building frenzy that occurred in Kentucky from about 1790 to 1810. Grimes Mill outlasted all of its neighbors as a business, being operated right up until the Great Depression, and endures today as a functioning facility—home of the Iroquois Hunt Club—and historic landmark. Through the decades, Grimes Mill matured and evolved with its various owners. The historic structure stands a lonely sentinel on the banks of Boone Creek, admitting to the curious eye little of its storied past. One must peer beyond the walls and peel away the layers of years. Only then do the stones begin to speak.

This book tells the story of an old mill, from its beginnings in the dim past to the present time. This is the story, not of an inanimate stone structure, but rather of the men and women who built and tended the mill, the various commercial enterprises carried on in its shadow, and the outside events that swirled around it. Early milling activities must be reconstructed from the meager resources available—old newspapers, deeds, wills, court order books, and such. More detailed investigation, analysis, and interpretation will be needed in order to fill in the canvas and complete the picture—to develop a comprehensive history of the milling industry in Fayette County. The author hopes that until that time, the present sketch of Grimes Mill will suffice.

The work is divided into seven sections. Chapter 1 defines the physical setting on Boone Creek and introduces the Grimes family. Chapter 2 details the process leading up to the mill's construction. Chapter 3 describes the mill-related structures as they were built and as they appear today. Chapter 4 covers the early years of mill operation (1807-1837), Chapter 5 the middle years (1837-1887), Chapter 6 the late years (1887-1928), and Chapter 7 the Iroquois Hunt Club years (1928 to present).

In transcribing nineteenth-century documents, only a few editorial changes were made and those only to improve readability. Capitalization was added at the beginning of sentences, punctuation and paragraphing were occasionally added, and some abbreviations were spelled out. Omissions of text are indicated by ellipses, and insertions are indicated by brackets.

In the course of preparing this book, the writer incurred many debts and wishes to acknowledge a few of those here. First of all, the work would never have gotten started without Larry Meadows, a director of the Red River Historical Society and Museum in Clay City. Larry's knowledge of local history and passion for milling in Kentucky is prodigious. He committed a considerable amount of time, energy, and information to this project, and his enthusiasm helped me see it through to the end.

I am also indebted to Nancy O'Malley, an archeologist at the University of Kentucky, where she is the assistant director of the W. S. Webb Museum of Anthropology and the Office of State Archaeology. Her scholarly work on milling in the state sets the standard for future researchers. My investigation of Grimes Mill began with the work she had done on the mill. I have benefited not only from her studies but also from her mentoring and her many ideas and suggestions.

Special thanks are due to Kevin Steele for producing the measured drawings; Eugene Peck and Debbie Young for clambering over, around and through the mill with tape measures, clipboards and flashlights helping gather data; Garland Dever for visiting the mill, milldam and quarries to examine the stone and for trying to teach me a little geology; Claire McCann, Lisa Carter and Gwen Curtis for outstanding assistance at the Special Collections and Map Collection, M. I. King Library, University of Kentucky; and Harkness Edwards, Jerry Hester, and the members of the Iroquois Hunt Club for encouraging this work, permitting access to the mill and grounds, and sharing archival materials from their collections.

I would like to acknowledge the following individuals for providing information, sharing resources, allowing access to property, and other good deeds: David and Cherry Fleischer, Joan Mayer, Bettie Kerr, Bobby Freeman, Jim Ringe, Rob Paratley,

Burgess Carey, Nora Lee Walters, Wallace Reed, Bettye Lee Mastin, Phyllis Spiker, Charles Hockensmith, Ted Hazen, Janice Van Natta, Diana McGinness, Russell Thompson, Neil Smith, and Julie Zapf. Lastly, I would like to thank my editor at Heritage Books, Roxanne Carlson, for her excellent work editing and designing the final version of the book.

While credit for the present work must be shared with many, the blame for mistakes and misinterpretations rests solely with the author.

Boone Creek Vicinity
circa 1807

The north-south road is Cleveland Road, which ran from Clevelands Landing to Paris in Bourbon County. The east-west road is the Lexington-Boonesborough Road (present day Athens-Boonesboro Road). The village of Cross Plains eventually gave way to Athens (laid out in 1836).

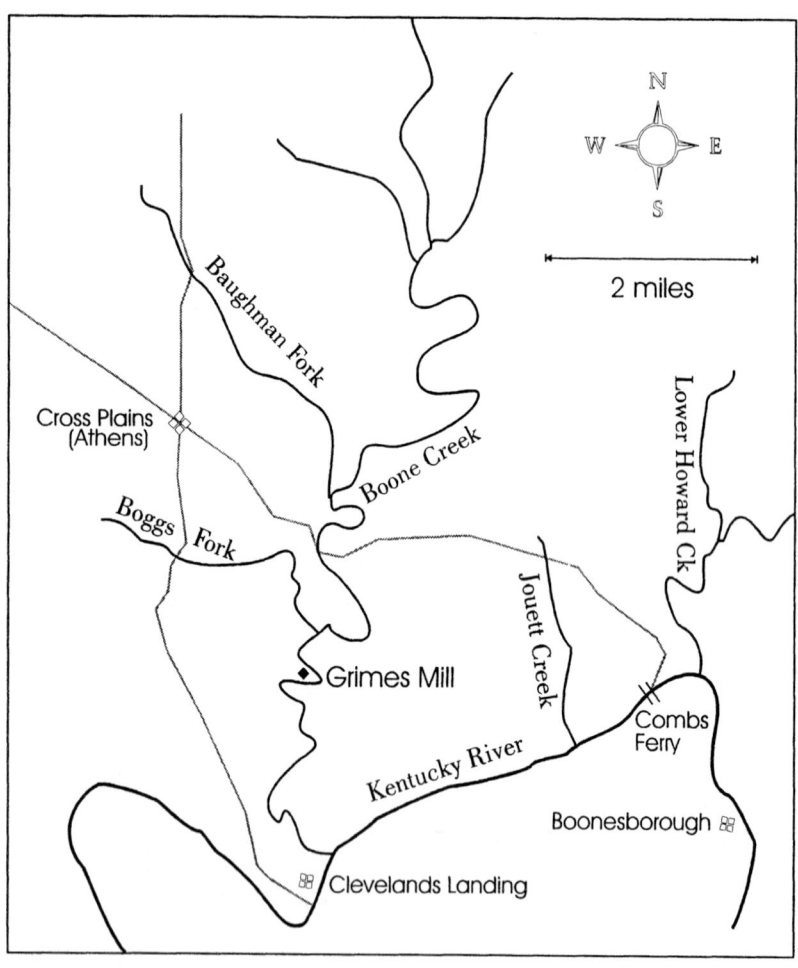

Chapter 1

Geographic and Historic Setting

The Grimes Mill setting is one of pristine beauty. To this area came the Grimes family from Virginia, settling first on the uplands, then descending to Boone Creek where they established a gristmill and numerous other business enterprises. This chapter serves as a brief introduction to the region and to the Grimes family.

The old mill may be seen by traveling southeast from Lexington on Richmond Road (US 25). Turn left on Grimes Mill Road and go down to Boone Creek, about 2 miles. The stone mill stands on the right side of the road, conspicuous by its striking red gables. The mill can also be reached by the Athens-Boonesboro Road (Ky 418). About 1 ½ miles past Athens, turn right on McCalls Mill Road and proceed another 1 ½ miles to the crossroads. Turn left on Grimes Mill Road and go down the hill to the mill.

Boone Creek

The mill is situated on Boone Creek where Grimes Mill Road crosses the stream, an area so lovely, it has been designated as one of Kentucky's "Scenic Byways."[1] The creek is noted for its steep cliffs, cascading waterfalls, and the variety of flora and fauna. Though rural and somewhat isolated today, the area was one of the early industrial centers in Kentucky. Located between Fort Boonesborough—the state's second permanent settlement—and Lexington, Boone Creek spawned a host of manufacturing establishments beginning in the 1790s.

Boone Creek is about ten miles long, as the crow flies, and flows generally from north to south. Its lower reaches form the boundary between Fayette County and Clark County. The headwaters of the creek are near the Lexington-Winchester Road (US 60), between Cleveland Road and Combs Ferry Road. Here it flows through rich soils of the Bluegrass plains, but progressing south the creek bisects an increasingly rugged landscape. The last few miles, the creek is lined with towering cliffs on both sides as it approaches confluence with the Kentucky River.

Boone Creek takes its name from Daniel Boone, the most prominent Kentucky pioneer to locate on its waters. The stream has been referred to by other names, but went by "Boone Creek" from a very early date. One version of how the creek was named appears in a court deposition:

> I was informed by Daniel Boone or some one else that the creek called Boone's creek that empties into the Kentucky River near Eli Cleaveland's took its name from the Indians taking Boone and his brother in law [John Stewart] in early times, before the country was settled, when they were trying to retake their horses from the Indians and being followed by them, ketched them on said creek.[2]

Two tributaries of Boone Creek also recall early settlers. Boggs Fork was named for Robert Boggs, who came out with the first surveyors in 1774, helped build Fort Boonesborough, and later made his home a few miles from Boone Creek. Baughman Fork[3] was named for the Boofman brothers, John and Jacob, who in 1776 were exploring up the stream and making "improvements" for land claims. Both brothers were later killed by Indians.[4]

In 1779, Daniel Boone built his stockaded fort on a branch of Baughman Fork. Although he eventually lost this land due to conflicting claims, Boone spent a few pleasant years here with his family and, no doubt, many enjoyable days hunting the nearby wooded hills. His occupancy of the station was brief. Boone lost the property when his claim was determined to be part of William Madison's 1,000-acre grant. In 1783, he moved to Marble Creek in Madison County. Boone's station site, now a state park, is located about one-half mile northeast of present-day Athens.[5]

The Athens community evolved from an earlier village known as Cross Plains. Its name derived from an ancient buffalo crossing and the "crossing-point of the hunters and troops passing to and fro between Harrodsburg, Lexington, Bryant's Station and Boonesborough."[6] Another vanished settlement, Cleveland's Landing, was located on the Kentucky River just below the mouth of Boone Creek. Here Eli Cleveland built a warehouse to store goods prior to loading on flatboats. He also had a boatyard where he built the vessels much in demand for shipping goods to New

Orleans and other markets.[7] His landing was accessible to much of Fayette County's rich tobacco crop and other produce. One of the first rural roads in the county went to Cleveland's Landing and is still in use today (Cleveland Road).[8] Cleveland owned several thousand acres of land on the lower reaches of Boone Creek, including the site where Grimes Mill would later be built.

Phillip Grimes

The Grimes family arrived on Boone Creek in the mid-1780s. They put down roots and passed many generations in the area before the name finally disappeared from the area. The progenitor of the Grimes family in Kentucky was Phillip Grimes, born 1734, the son of Nicholas Grimes. Phillip grew up in Prince William County, Virginia, in an area that later became Loudoun County. The Grimes family, though not prominent in local politics, included some of the largest landowners in the county. They lived in the area south of present-day Leesburg, Virginia, about 30 miles west of Washington, D.C.[9]

During the French and Indian War, Phillip was out on the Virginia frontier as a sergeant in the militia. The county awarded him 330 pounds of tobacco for his services.[10] Phillip married Mary Dowdall, and they raised eight children, all born in Virginia. Phillip and his brother, Nicholas Jr., were named executors of their father's will. Nicholas Jr. inherited his father's plantation.[11]

Phillip Grimes left his homeplace sometime after the Revolutionary War and settled with his family in Fayette County, Kentucky. He was listed as a taxpayer of Cameron Parish, Loudoun County, for the last time in 1783 and probably moved to Kentucky shortly thereafter.[12] Phillip's name later showed up in a list of claims made by British citizens for debts owed to Loyalist merchants at the time of the Revolutionary War. A petition against Phillip, dated 1800, stated that "Philip Grimes of Loudoun... removed to Kentucky about twenty years ago; [was] then solvent."[13]

Phillip probably came out to Kentucky several times before making the move permanent. He may have been here in May 1780, when "Phillip Grymes" by virtue of treasury warrants entered two adjoining tracts on Stoner Creek, at that time in Kentucky County, Virginia. One entry was for 1,500 acres, the other for 1,600 acres.[14] His Loudoun County neighbor, John Payne, surveyed the land in

December 1783. Phillip did not participate in the surveys, but his son John Grimes was one of the chainmen. Phillip was awarded a grant for his Stoner Creek land, located in present-day Clark County.[15]

Phillip Grimes can be documented as a Kentucky resident by 1787, when he was listed on the first tax rolls for Fayette County along with his son James.[16] Grimes did not settle on his Stoner Creek property, which was about five miles northeast of present-day Winchester. He located instead in the vicinity of Cross Plains (present-day Athens) in southeastern Fayette County, near the Winn family and other former neighbors from Virginia.[17]

For his homeplace, Phillip purchased 225 acres from Robert Boggs.[18] Boggs had acquired this tract on Baughman Fork, a tributary on the west side of Boone Creek, by virtue of a Virginia land grant. Phillip probably settled on this land when he moved to Kentucky, as he was listed on the tax rolls each year among the same family groups from 1787 until his death in 1806. Phillip's plantation was located near the headwaters of Baughman Fork, about two miles northwest of Athens near the intersection of Athens-Boonesboro Road and Interstate 75.[19]

The father helped his adult children locate in this area. Phillip sold half of his plantation to his eldest son, John. Three other sons—Benjamin, James, and Charles—also bought property and settled nearby. The 1804 county tax rolls listed Valinda Grimes, John's widow, with 112 acres, James Grimes with 270, Benjamin Grimes with 100, and "Phillip Grimes & Son [Charles]" with 173.[20] Sons Stephen and Avory located a few miles north, in what is now the Clintonville area of Bourbon County.

After the turn of the century, Phillip was aging and few records exist to document his activities. He did leave one trail in Fayette circuit court, indicating that he joined in the popular Kentucky pastime of citizens suing their neighbors. Phillip's Stoner Creek property was threatened by several competing claims. Most ominous was the interference caused by Charles Morgan's 1,000-acre preemption. In 1801, Phillip filed suit against Morgan to settle the boundary question. Neither man would live to see the case settled. A number of interlocutory orders were issued—all in the Grimeses' favor, but each was contested and the case dragged on. Final judgment was not rendered until 1820, by which time the suit was styled as *Phillip Grimes' heirs vs. Charles Morgan's heirs.* Sadly, for the Grimes family, it turned out to be twenty years of futility.

Grimes earlier had lost part of his 1,500-acre tract to Enoch Smith, because it was not surveyed precisely according to the entry. Following the Supreme Court's decision against him, Grimes had his 1,600-acre tract resurveyed, so that he would not lose it too. In *Grimes vs. Morgan*, the court found fault with the new survey made "on entirely different ground, and this without any apology for so doing."

> This court reluctantly disturbs the acts of its preceptor, and would still more unwillingly do so on a mere difference of opinion. And it is to be regretted that this cause has progressed to such an extent, with no doubt increased expectations in the complainants and considerable costs on both sides.... This conduct [Grimes' resurvey] must be fatal to the claim. It is therefore decreed and ordered that the interlocutory decree heretofore made in this suit be set aside, and the complainants bill be dismissed, and that they pay to the defendants their costs herein expended.[21]

Phillip lived on his Baughman Fork plantation until his death in 1806. His will directed that the Stoner Creek property be divided among sons James, Benjamin, Avory, and the heirs of deceased son Stephen. He devised to son Charles "the tract of land on which I live containing 112 ½ acres."[22] At the time of his father's death, Charles Grimes was already in the milling business on Boggs Fork and was at work on plans to construct a mill on Boone Creek.

Charles Grimes

Charles Grimes was born in Loudoun County, Virginia, in 1771.[23] He married Jane Winn, one of nine daughters of Owen Winn of Fayette County. In 1792, Charles was listed on the Fayette County tax rolls as the owner of two slaves, two horses, three cattle, and no land. Charles and Jane returned to Virginia briefly, then came back to live on his father's plantation.[24]

Fayette court records provide a trail of Charles' activities for the next few years. In 1803, he proved George Winn's will at court. In 1804, Charles was appointed captain for the 8th regiment of the Kentucky militia and was one of the men appointed to view John McCall's proposed mill site and assess damages. In 1806, he served on a jury trial with his brothers, Benjamin and James Grimes, and John Winn Jr. and with his brother James served as executor of his father's will. In 1808, he proved the will of Susanna Lucas and gave a security bond for Squire Boone, who was appointed guardian of Randall Noe's children. In 1811, he gave a security bond for Henry C. Clay, who was appointed guardian of Samuel Clay's children, and another security bond for Henry Moore, who was granted a tavern license. In 1816, he provided the surety for Henry C. Clay to marry Mary Grimes, who was Charles' sister.[25] Although this is only a small sample of his activities during the period, it is sufficient to show that Charles Grimes was becoming a figure of some importance in his neighborhood.

Though many of Charles' actions may be discerned from public records, these are usually lacking in character and personality. The papers accompanying court cases, however, often supply such personal touches, and the Grimeses, like most of their neighbors, appeared in court quite frequently. One instance, a family matter, involved three brothers—Charles, James, and Stephen. Some time after their father's death, the family quarreled over a slave devised by Phillip's will to the heirs of Stephen, Phillip's deceased son. James brought suit on behalf of Stephen's children against Charles, who would not give up the slave, named Dinah. One of the depositions taken on Charles' behalf recalled an incident that occurred at his house north of Athens, where he was living in 1795.

> [W]e have met at the house of Mrs. Winn on the 16th day of August 1810 to take the Deposition of Mrs. Winn....
>
> The deposition of Mary Winn [Owen Winn's widow] who being duly sworn deposeth and Saith that about fourteen or fifteen years ago I happened at Charles Grimes's and when I was there my Daughter, Charles Grimes's wife, took me to a Kitchen where an old negro woman had [given birth

> to] two children. And soon after We got there, old Mr. Philip Grimes came into the Kitchen where we were and immediately Says to me Did you ever see such poor little Babes as these are.... And afterwards he immediately said that he had gave the two little children to Jenny, the wife of Charles Grimes, if she could raise them, But says he, I don't think she [can].
>
> Question by Charles Grimes. Did you think at that time that them children could be raised. [In other words, would they live?]
>
> Answer. I was doubtfull whether they could be raised or not.

According to the testimony of the midwife, Mrs. Catherine Cade, she was called "to attend a negro woman at the house of Charles Grimes in child bed." After being there some time, "the said negro was delivered of two children, and I took particular notice of the children, and they were very Small and poor [probably premature], which children was afterwards called Dinah and Harry." She remarked that the woman was "much advanced in years and illy able to raise two children."

> Question by Charles Grimes. Do you not conceive that the negroes that I have now in my possession called Dinah and Harry were the same negroes that you have before alluded to.
>
> Answer. Yes I do.[26]

The case is valuable in that it provides a glimpse, albeit grim, inside the home of Charles Grimes. The case also reminds us of a darker reality, the fact that slaves were treated as property and that courts frequently were called upon to settle disputes involving slave ownership.

Three of the Grimes brothers—Benjamin, James, and Charles—prospered in their multifarious business interests in Fayette County. While they lived near each other in the Boone Creek area, they mostly went their separate ways in business. They pursued similar opportunities, but seldom as partners. Each made his mark in a different manner. Charles Grimes made his in the flouring industry. Grimes Mill on Boone Creek would establish him as one of the major players in this arena. His first venture in the field, however, was a mill on Boggs Fork. In 1804, Charles advertised "Mills For Sale" in the *Kentucky Gazette*:

> I have for sale a Water Grist overshot Mill with two pair of stones and 17 feet [water] wheel, and a Saw Mill, on Boggs's Fork, waters of Boone's creek, one mile and a half from the Cross-Plains in Fayette county. Also a Mill with one pair of stones, which will go either by water or horses; about forty acres of land on which the Mills stand, will be sold with them.... For terms apply to the subscriber, about two miles from the above mills.
>
> Charles Grimes[27]

The description of the mill as 1 ½ miles from Cross Plains pinpoints the location on Boggs Fork, if accurate, as 1 mile from the mouth of Boone Creek. When Charles obtained this property, from whom, and to whom he sold it are not known. What is clear is that during this period Charles Grimes was already involved, in some fashion, in the milling business.

John Winn Jr.

John Winn Jr. was connected to the Grimes family by marriage. He was Charles Grimes' brother-in-law. Charles Grimes' wife, Jane, was John Winn's sister.[28] The Winn family came to Kentucky around the same time as the Grimeses. Both were resident by 1787 and appeared on the first Fayette County tax rolls. The three Winn brothers—Owen, George, and Thomas—had adjoining tracts surveyed for them on the waters of Stoner Creek in 1784.[29] Their property was very near Phillip Grimes' land in what would later become Clark County. Like the Grimes family, the Winns chose to settle in southeastern Fayette County, since Stoner Creek was considered a wilderness area at that time.

John Winn Jr. was Charles Grimes' partner in the mill venture. Together they would purchase a 60-acre tract on Boone Creek where they intended to put up a gristmill.[30] In contrast to his illustrious partner, John is a rather obscure, little-known figure.

However, he played a prominent role in county affairs until his untimely death in 1817.

John Winn Jr. was born about 1779, the son of Owen Winn. John married Susanna Dulin, daughter of Thaddeus Dulin.[31] John and his wife lived on a plantation on Boggs Fork near Athens. They started out with 70 acres "on the cross plains" that John obtained from his father.[32] At the time of his death, John had increased his holdings to 350 acres.

Many of John's activities may be discerned from the county records. In 1800, he was appointed lieutenant for the 8th regiment of the Kentucky militia and in 1803 was promoted to captain of the regiment. In the year 1806, John gave security bond for John Hendley, who was granted a tavern license "at the cross plains," provided the surety for his sister Barbara Winn to marry Robert Bush, was appointed "Inspector of Tobacco" for Cleveland's warehouse, and served on a jury that viewed the site for William Christian's gristmill. In 1807, John was appointed with Thomas Clark and James Spurr to appraise the personal estate of Richard Vallandingham and was appointed with William Davenport and Thomas Clark to view a road from near Boone's Station Meeting House to intersect with the road to Cleveland's Landing. This road ran through the land of Lettice Winn, widow of George Winn. Also that year, John was promoted to major of the 1st battalion, 8th regiment of the Kentucky militia. He was one of four men ordered to examine the accounts and settle the estate of Nicholas Curry in 1812. He was appointed guardian of his sister Polly King's children in 1813. Also that year, the governor appointed John an "Inspector of Flour" for Cleveland's warehouse. He was named executor of his father-in-law Thaddeus Dulin's estate in 1814.[33] Only a representative sample of John Winn's activities has been included here. From this list it is clear that he was a man of growing influence in his neighborhood.

John Winn Jr. died in 1817 when he was only thirty-eight years old. In October of that year, the court ordered "An inventory of Appraisement of the Estate of Major John Winn deceased." John's wife, Susanna, was the administrator.[34]

Chapter 2

Charles Grimes Builds A Mill

T he most readily available contemporary account leading to the construction of Grimes Mill is the record left by John Winn Jr. and Charles Grimes in the county court order books. Tracing these records, one can establish with some certainty the basic facts regarding the mill's origin. What's missing are the personalities and human touches that bring the story to life. A few of these are provided by the historical tradition associated with Grimes Mill.

Historical Tradition

A popular version of Grimes Mill's history attributes the Boone Creek establishment to Phillip Grimes:

> The mill was built for Philip Grimes in 1803 by a crew of Irish builders and stone workers, captained by one Peter Paul.[1]

This rendering of the Grimes Mill story has gained considerable currency through repetition in numerous newspaper articles, magazines, books, and a handbook for members of the Iroquois Hunt Club.[2] A more elaborate version of the mill's beginnings appeared in another article:

> Philip Grimes... was a man of some consequence with a far-sighted idea of business and while he was building his original home, a log house, above the bend in the stream on the road from the Richmond pike, he saw the value of the never-failing stream of water, and sending to New England for an Irish contractor and builder named Peter Paul, who came to Kentucky with a crew of thirty Irish stone workers, he built a dam across it and erected in 1803 what is still known as Grimes' Mill.[3]

The origin of this tradition is uncertain. One possible source is John Gourlay of the Iroquois Hunt Club, who authored an article on the mill in the *Lexington Herald* on February 21, 1929.[4]

Peter Paul could have been contracted to build the mill. He was a stoneworker and was in Lexington by 1802. That year, "Peter Paul & Son, stonecutters from London," placed an ad in the newspaper for their business near Lexington.[5] For a brief biography of Peter Paul and a discussion of his possible role in the mill's construction, see Appendix E.

Fayette circuit court records indicate that the mill was not erected in 1803 and that it was not built for Phillip. There is no evidence that Phillip owned any property on Boone Creek or built a home near the mill site. His residence was four miles away, up around the headwaters of Baughman Fork, as documented above. The gristmill was actually the work of Phillip's son, Charles Grimes, and a partner, John Winn Jr.

Since the traditional version of the mill's beginning has been repeated so frequently and in such a variety of publications, the evidence for Charles Grimes being the builder of the mill, at a later date than 1803, is presented below in considerable detail.

There is at least one published account that does attribute the mill to Charles Grimes. The reference appears in William Perrin's history of Fayette County, in a chapter on the Athens Precinct:

> Charles Grimes built one of the early mills, which
> became the property of his sons at his death.[6]

Although Perrin does not say so, evidence suggests that this was Grimes Mill on Boone Creek, the only mill Charles left to his sons, Charles W. and Carlo Grimes. The statement was written while Charles W. and Carlo were still living, which lends additional credence to Perrin's version.

Winn and Grimes Mill

John Winn Jr. and Charles Grimes formulated plans to construct a gristmill on Boone Creek. They found an ideal location in a large bend of the creek and purchased the site from Eli Cleveland, by deed dated May 4, 1805. The place they selected for their mill was about two miles from the Kentucky River. They paid Cleveland 50 pounds for the property described as containing "sixty acres and thirty poles by survey... Laying on Boons Creek in the County of Fayette."[7]

The mill seat was on Cleveland's 250-acre grant on Boone Creek and Boggs Fork. This tract was first claimed by James Neavill, for whom it was surveyed. Neavill then assigned his "Right & title" to Cleveland, to whom the grant was issued.[8] Cleveland in turn sold a portion of the tract to Winn and Grimes.

The same month they bought the Boone Creek land, Winn and Grimes petitioned the Fayette circuit court for permission to build a gristmill:

> On the motion of John Winn and Charles Grimes *for leave to build a water grist mill* on Boons Creek in the county of Fayette they owning the lands on both sides of said creek *where the said mill is proposed to be built*; Ordered that a writ of ad quod damnum issue, to be executed according to law on the 28th Instant, and return thereof made to Court according to law.[9] (emphasis added)

The phrase "where the said mill is proposed to be built" indicates that in 1805 the mill had not yet been erected.

Mill building followed a well-choreographed procedure based on centuries-old English law. The Kentucky version of the law required the owner to obtain permission to erect a dam from the county court of jurisdiction. The owner initiated this process by petitioning the court for a writ of *ad quod damnum*. This writ was an order directing the sheriff to empanel a jury of twelve citizens to view the mill site and determine what damages might arise from construction of the dam. Jurors were instructed

> to examine the lands above and below... which may probably overflow, and say to what damage it will be of the several proprietors, and whether the mansion house of any such proprietor, or the offices, curtelages [yards] or gardens... or orchards will be overflowed; to enquire whether... fish of passage or ordinary navigation will be obstructed; whether [and] by what means such obstruction may

be prevented; and whether in their opinion, the health of the neighbours will be annoyed by the stagnation of the waters.[10]

After the jury returned its report, the court issued a summons to anyone whose land the dam was likely to damage. These proprietors were ordered to come to court "to shew cause why the party applying should not have leave to build his said mill and dam."[11]

Winn and Grimes suffered numerous delays getting their mill seat approved, some of which were their own doing. First, it turned out that they only owned land on the west side of the creek, not both sides. At the June session of court, they entered their corrected mill petition, and added a sawmill to the request. In August, the court issued summonses to Adam Winn and William Ford. They were to appear at the next court session to give their reasons, if any, why the mill "may not be established."[12]

The jury's findings were returned to court in October, and Winn and Grimes moved to quash the report, "they refusing to build their mill on the conditions mentioned therein."[13] Perhaps, the young entrepreneurs found the terms for erecting the dam unacceptable or the award for damages too high. In November, Winn and Grimes reentered their petition, which provides some further detail. The court ordered a jury to meet on Boone Creek

> for the purpose of assessing damages and condemning one acre of land the property of William Ford *against which land they wish to abut a dam for working a water grist mill,* they owning the land on the other side of said creek, and make report thereof to Court.[14] (emphasis added)

Ford's land was on the Clark County side of the creek. Due to the public benefit of gristmills, courts were empowered to condemn land, usually one acre, for the dam abutment when a petitioner only owned on one side of the stream.[15] The reference to Ford's land "against which land they wish to abut a dam" is a clear indication that the dam had not been put up at that time.

Grimes Mill Tract
circa 1807

Eli Cleveland sold this tract "containing 60 acres and 30 poles" to John Winn Jr. and Charles Grimes in 1805. Neighbors, taken from deeds and court orders, included William Cotton, James Bentley, John Poindexter, Mrs. Bibb (widow of David Bibb), John McCall, and John Morgan.

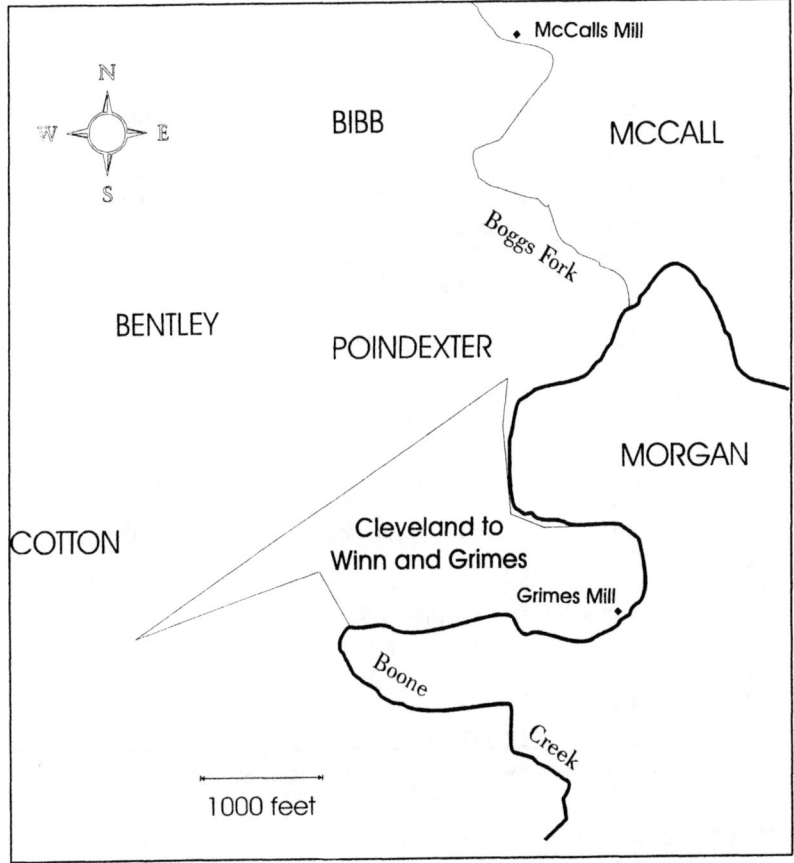

Boone Creek Land Grants

Land grants were plotted using "metes and bounds" and other property descriptions in the original surveys. Interfering grants (for example, Daniel Boone's station tract) were omitted for clarity. Due to conflicting calls and other survey errors, locations are only approximate.

No.	Acreage	Granted to	Old Virginia Grants, Volume:Page
1	442	Eli Cleveland	9:230
2	740	Alexander Cleveland	6:247
3	400	Alexander Cleveland	6:223
4	260	Alexander Cleveland	6:248
5	**250**	**Eli Cleveland*[1]**	**2:289[3]**
Logan	200	Nicholas Curry[2]	6:47
6	907	William Gillespie	1:68
7	400	William Gillespie	1:68
8	400	Robert Boggs	1:116
9	**276**	**Robert Boggs****	**13:319**
10	400	Christinah Boffman[4]	9:272
11	1,000	Christinah Boffman[4]	6:298
12	1,300	Charles Morgan	11:302
13	250	Richard Wade	14:150
14	250	Leonard K. Bradley[5]	15:103
15	1,000	William Madison	6:21
16	245	Robert Sanders	4:374
17	500	John Niblick[6]	10:204
18	1,845	William Triplett	15:82
19	2,000	James Hickman	6:49
20	1,000	William Robinson	12:407
21	400	David Robinson	1:107
22	1,000	David Robinson	1:353
23	1,000	David Robinson	1:107
24	240	John Floyd's heirs	19:249
25	316	John Floyd's heirs	13:530
26	400	John Floyd's heirs	13:516
27	684	John Floyd's heirs	13:521
x	246	John Floyd's heirs	14:174

*Charles Grimes and John Winn Jr. purchased 60 acres and 30 poles of Cleveland's grant for their mill seat.

**Phillip Grimes purchased 225 acres of Boggs' grant for his homeplace.

Notes: (1) Surveyed for James Neavill; (2) surveyed for Benjamin Logan; placement uncertain; (3) Old Kentucky Grants; (4) surveyed for John Boffman; (5) surveyed for Richard Wade; and (6) surveyed for Daniel Boone.

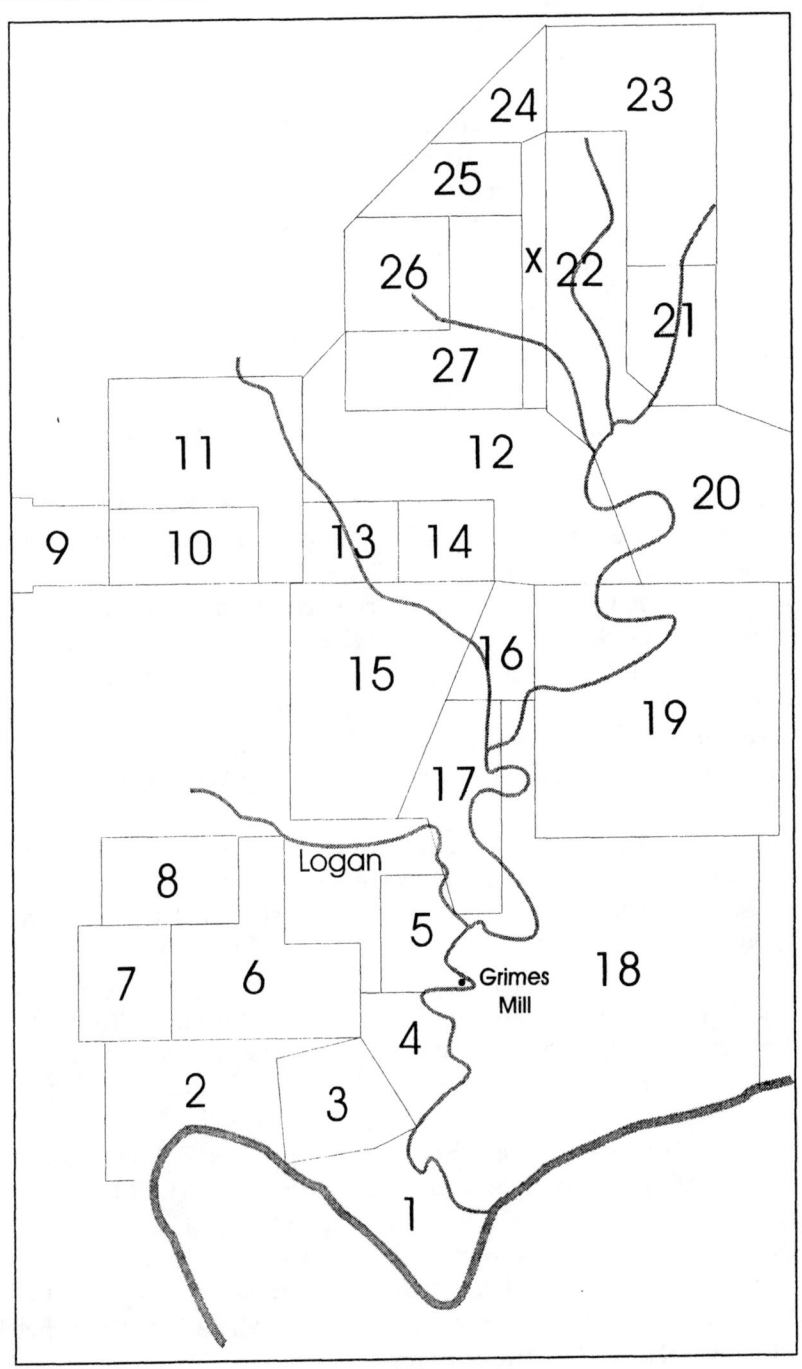

The year 1805 ended with no report of the jury's findings, nor were any orders recorded in 1806. Finally, in March 1807, Winn and Grimes petitioned the court for their mill yet again and another writ was issued. The petition stated that Winn and Grimes "are desirous of erecting a dam to work a water Grist mill on Boons creek," indicating that in March 1807 they still had not put their dam across Boone Creek. A jury was ordered to meet at the site in April to make their inquiries.[16]

The jury's "Report of Inquest" on Winn's and Grimes' mill was returned to court in April, but for some reason was not recorded. William Winn was summoned to appear at the next court and show cause why the mill and dam "may not be established agreeable to the report of the Jury." The case was continued in May. Then for some unexplained reason, the court did not get around to formally establishing the mill (i.e., recording its approval in the order book) for three and a half years.[17]

Finally, in October 1810, the jury's report was approved by the court and recorded. According to the report, the twelve jurors met on April 4, 1807, at the Boone Creek property where Winn and Grimes "desire erecting a Damm for the purpose of working a water grist and Saw Mills." For one end of the milldam, still not built at that date, the jury laid off one acre on William Winn's land across the creek, on the Clark County side, valued at seven dollars. They determined that a dam of five feet ten inches to six feet high would not damage any of the neighboring property by flooding. The record states that William Winn gave consent, and the mill was established.[18]

There are a number of possible reasons for the lengthy process and numerous delays involved in the establishment of Winn and Grimes mill. Unfortunately, due to the absence of records bearing on the issue, it is not possible to provide a satisfactory explanation at this time.

The disparity between the time of the jury's favorable report (April 1807) and the court's recording of the report (October 1810) makes it difficult to fix the exact date the mill was put into operation. Construction most likely was completed sometime between April 1807 and April 1808. In the latter month, Charles Grimes petitioned the county court for a "New Road" to be opened "to the mill of said Charles Grimes."[19]

Evidence indicates that the mill was constructed before final approval was recorded by the court. That was not unusual. Many instances can be found where mills were built without ever being approved by the court, or at least without approval being recorded in the court order books. That does not imply, however, that those owners ignored the law. The requirement for mill builders to obtain a writ of *ad quod damnum* from the county court were well known, and anyone erecting a dam without following this process would almost certainly end up in a lawsuit or worse. If the petitioner filed for a writ, and following that the jury visited the site, assessed the damages, marked one acre across the stream and affixed its value, and made its report, then the intent of the law was satisfied. If, subsequently, all affected parties were agreeable to the dam being built, then there were no more issues for the court to decide. At that point, recording the court's approval in the order book was merely a formality.

The evidence presented above leaves little doubt that the mill now standing on Boone Creek and known as Grimes Mill was built for Charles Grimes in 1807. This finding cannot be reconciled with the tradition that Philip Grimes built the mill in 1803. It is not hard to imagine the oral history undergoing small changes over the years. An account that the mill was "built by Phillip Grimes' son" could have evolved in time to "built by Phillip Grimes." Of course, there remains the possibility that Phillip Grimes actually did build an earlier mill at the location. It could have been a smaller, more primitive affair that was replaced by Charles Grimes' mill. There is no hard evidence for an earlier mill, but the court order books that could prove it were destroyed by fire in 1803. On the whole, however, it seems unlikely that Phillip at age sixty-nine left his Baughman Fork plantation and moved down to Boone Creek to build a gristmill.[20]

Winn a Brief Partner

The establishment on Boone Creek has gone by the name of Grimes Mill ever since it was built. After 1807, it was never again referred to as Winn and Grimes Mill. One might ask what happened to Grimes' partner, John Winn Jr. Winn and Grimes purchased the land as tenants in common. There is no deed recorded for Winn conveying his share to Grimes. Winn, as a favor to his brother-in-law, may have added his name to the endeavor in order to cull political support for the project. Or the two may have had an agreement calling for Grimes to pay back Winn's investment.

The most likely explanation for Winn's role is one of the following scenarios: Grimes put up all the purchase money for the property, and Winn was a partner in name only. Or Winn sold his interest in the mill tract to Grimes shortly after they bought it, and the deed was simply not recorded. Charles must have had a good title, as there was no challenge when C. W. and Carlo Grimes inherited the property following Charles' death.

Whatever their arrangement, Winn was never an active partner in Grimes Mill's operation. In fact, John had a mill of his own on Boggs Fork. One of James Hawkins' corners referred to in a deed was a "walnut stump on a hill side below John Winns mill-dam." The dam was located about a mile southwest of Athens.[21] No other information on Winn's mill is available.

Chapter 3

Mill Construction:
An Architectural Review

The construction of Grimes Mill was a complex and difficult project that must have tested the mettle of its designers, craftsmen, and laborers. The builders are unknown but would have included a skilled stonemason and millwright. The first city directory for Lexington, dated 1806, identifies seven who practiced the stone crafts. One of these was Peter Paul, stonecutter, traditionally credited as the builder of Grimes Mill. Additional information about Peter Paul is provided in Appendix E.

The majority of the construction work had to be performed in a remote area with primitive tools and local resources. The first task was to select the site and plan the mill layout. After a suitable quarry was located and opened, stonemasons cut, hauled, dressed, and laid the stone. Trees were felled, sawed and hewn for posts, beams, planking, and shingles, which carpenters used to install the framing, floors, and roof. While Peter Paul could have been responsible for the stone work, the mill machinery had to be constructed by an experienced millwright. Some of the mechanical parts may have been purchased—the millstones, for example—but most were probably fabricated on site by a millwright, including the water wheel, axles and gears, and a host of other mill-related parts. The dam was erected, the millrace dug, and water-controlling gates installed at both ends of the race. The present condition of the mill suggests that these tasks were performed well. Mill terminology used here is further explained in the Glossary (Appendix A).

In order to describe the mill design and construction accurately, extensive measurements and numerous photographs were taken on the inside and outside of the building. Similar measurements were made for other features in the mill complex, including the millrace and dam. The site plan was then plotted on a topographic map, and a series of measured drawings was prepared for the gristmill.[1] For discussion purposes, the site may be divided into three functional parts: the dam, millrace, and mill. These are described as they look today and as they might have existed at the time the mill was built.

Milldam

The milldam served two major functions. It raised the water level several feet above its normal height in the creek, which increased the potential energy available to the mill. The dam created a millpond, which stored water for use by the mill. Water from the millpond could be released as needed and directed to the mill's water wheel via the millrace. The available head (vertical distance the water falls) and the volume of water flow determined the energy available to power the mill. While the dam provided part of the head, additional head was provided by the difference in elevation between the dam and the mill. Steeply dropping streams like Boone Creek provided ideal mill sites.

The amount of work a mill can do is related to its horsepower.[2] Mill builders sought locations along streams where a high head and a large, steady water flow were available. The greater the head, the greater the power—and the larger the diameter wheel needed to harness the power. The greater the water flow directed to the wheel, the greater the power—and the wider the wheel and the larger the buckets needed to catch the water.

The dam for Grimes Mill was erected across Boone Creek, near the present highway bridge. The remnant of a dam abutment is still standing on the Fayette County side of the creek, about 150 feet upstream from the bridge, at the base of a steeply rising hill. Although this remnant could be original, it is difficult to assume so, since parts of the dam must have been repaired or rebuilt numerous times after floods. There is no trace of an abutment on the opposite bank. The Clark County side is in the flood plain and is where most of the millpond would have been. The top of the dam remnant is 7 feet above the stream bed. According to the jury's report to the county court in 1807, a dam up to 6 feet high was to be allowed at the site. The estimated length of the dam is 100 feet, the horizontal distance from the top of the abutment across the creek to the opposite bank.

The design of the dam may be inferred from the remnant. It was constructed of locally quarried stone laid in two parallel walls perpendicular to the stream. Each wall is about 2 ½ feet thick, and the 9-foot space between the two walls is filled with stone rubble. Walls and rubble are capped with a veneer of concrete, which is clearly not original.[3]

Millrace

Water from the millpond was carried to the water wheel via the millrace—an artificial channel that was usually dug by hand and lined with wood. There were adjustable openings, called gates, at either end of the millrace. These could be opened to allow water to flow or closed to hold it back. The head gate at the upper end was used to control the flow of water from the millpond to the millrace. At the lower end of the millrace, water was directed to a wooden sluice, or sluice box, and water flow was controlled by a sluice gate. The sluice carried water to the top of the water wheel, where it was discharged, causing the wheel to turn. This type of water wheel was called an "overshot wheel."

At Grimes Mill, the distance from the head gate to the mill is approximately 850 feet. Although now mostly filled in, the path of the millrace is still evident. About half of the race can be seen in a 1929 photograph.[4] The millrace began at the southwest corner of the millpond, where the head gate was located at the dam abutment. The opening for the head gate—just over 3 feet wide—is clearly defined at the end of two stone walls, which form part of the millrace. At the head gate opening, for the first 20 feet or so of the race, the stone walls and base remain, and approximately 250 feet of the original channel of the race is visible. From there, the millrace ran "with the stone quarry," as mentioned in an 1863 deed,[5] then under the road to the mill. The stone outcrop of the old quarry can be detected in places, below where the hunt club's kennels are today.

A portion of the millrace can still be detected on the south side of the road. Though covered with fill, the tops of the stone walls of the race are just visible. This segment of the race is about 4 ½ feet wide and runs from the road a distance of about 60 feet toward the mill. The 1929 photograph shows this segment continuing another 40 feet to the archway at the mill, where a wooden sluice would have carried the water on to the water wheel. The photograph also indicates that there may have been another gate near the road, where water could be diverted from the millrace back to the creek.

Although the gate is not visible, a ditch-like channel can be seen in the area now occupied by the Hunt Club's propane tank.

Grimes Mill had its water wheel inside the mill, where it was protected from the elements. The sluice ran through the archway in the north wall of the mill and over to the top of the water wheel. Water from the buckets of the turning water wheel emptied into the wheel pit. Water in the wheel pit ran out under an archway in the south wall to a tailrace that flowed down to Boone Creek. There is no visible trace of the tailrace today, and the archway in the south wall is covered by fill.

Gristmill

Inside the gristmill, a set of gear works transferred power from the rotating water wheel. This power was used not only to turn the millstones but also to drive other mill-related machinery, such as elevators, cleaners, conveyors, bolters (sifters), and hoists.

Grimes Mill stands on the west bank of Boone Creek. Structures built in the flood plain have to be able to withstand the destructive forces of flood waters. Wall discoloration inside indicates that it is not uncommon for the basement floor to be covered by a foot or two of water. That the structure survived nearly two hundred years of periodic flooding attests to that fact that the mill was not only well built, but also well sited.

The mill, though properly described as two-and-a-half stories high, actually has four working levels: the basement, first and second floors, and the attic. The walls of the first three levels are constructed from stone blocks laid in regular horizontal courses. Based on the average-size stone and the total volume of the walls, somewhere in the neighborhood of 10,000 cut stones were used in the mill's construction. The 1 foot by 2 foot by 5 foot blocks in the basement wall weigh over 1,600 pounds apiece.

Two different building stones were used. One is the whitish-colored stone from the Tyrone Formation known as birdseye limestone, referred to from here on as "Tyrone Limestone." Many of its faces display hollowed out, spherical ("subconchoidal") fractures that are characteristic of the stone. The other stone, from the Oregon Formation, is called Kentucky River Marble, a tan to grayish dolomite containing variable amounts of limestone. Iron present in the dolomite gives this stone its buff-colored appearance.

Site Plan

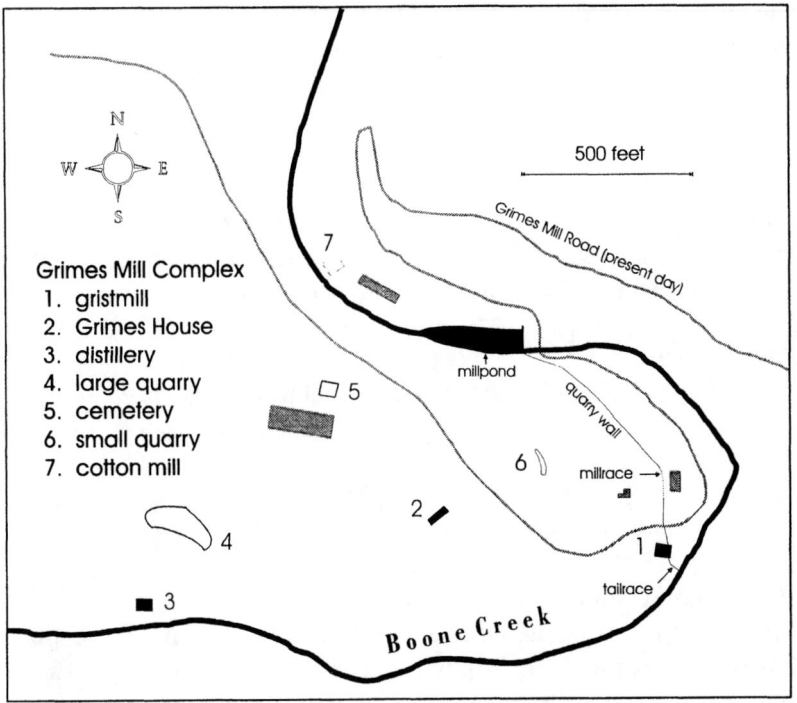

The dam, millrace, and gristmill are shown in relation to present-day Grimes Mill Road. Location of the sawmill is unknown. The cotton mill may have been in the area of the shaded rectangle on the north (Clark County) side of Boone Creek. There was a road to the distillery (not shown). The shaded rectangles are modern structures.

Measured Drawings

These following plans were made from actual measurements taken inside and outside the mill. Drawings correspond to the mill's appearance in the nineteenth century, and thus many modern features (such as the porch on the south side) are omitted. A fifty-foot scale is included with each drawing.

A. Floor Plans
No internal partitions (rooms) are shown, since none can be inferred for the original mill. The four small squares in the center of each floor represent the location of support posts.

B. Elevations
The door on the right side of the east elevation has been filled in with stone. The south façade has undergone major changes; the soil level was raised to support the porch addition, the small arch was covered by fill, and a window on the first floor was enlarged to make a door to the porch.

C. Cross Sections
Front view shows the post and beam construction of the three working floors and a king-post truss in the attic. Back view shows the sluice box, which carried water through the archway in the north wall, to the overshot water wheel. The wheel pit was excavated to a greater depth than the basement in order to accommodate the water wheel.

FLOOR PLANS

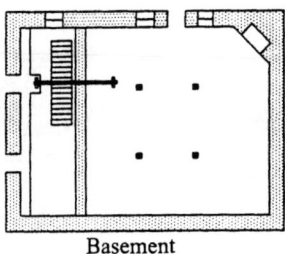

Basement

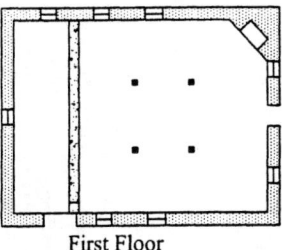

First Floor

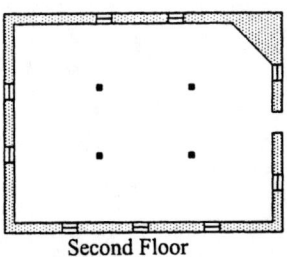

Second Floor

0 10 20 30 40 50

Drawings by: G. Kevin Steele

ELEVATIONS

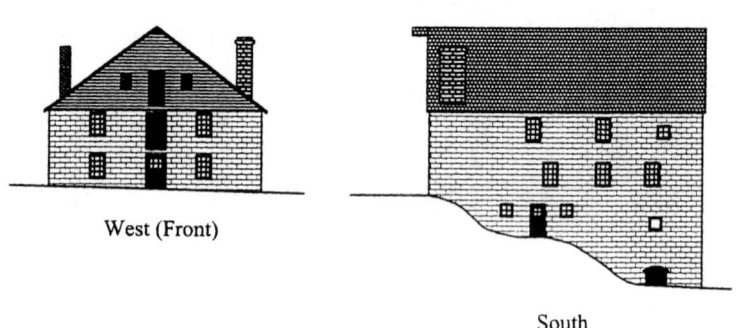

West (Front)

South

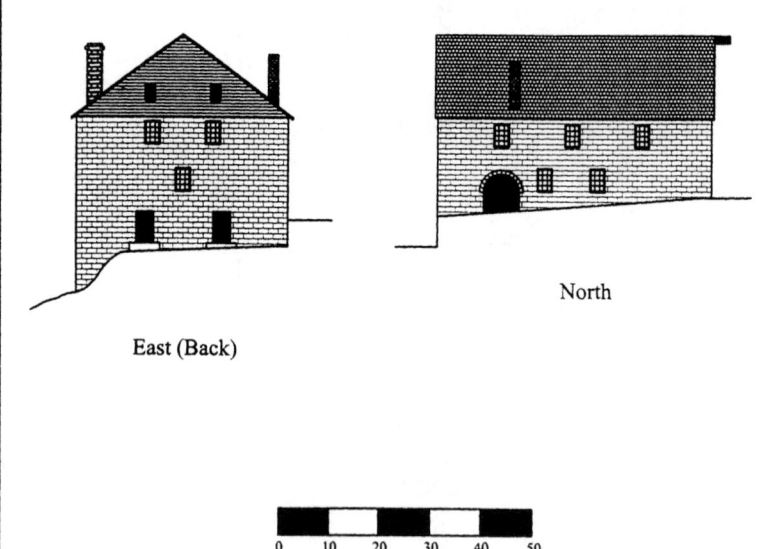

East (Back)

North

0 10 20 30 40 50

Drawings by: G. Kevin Steele

CROSS SECTIONS

Front View

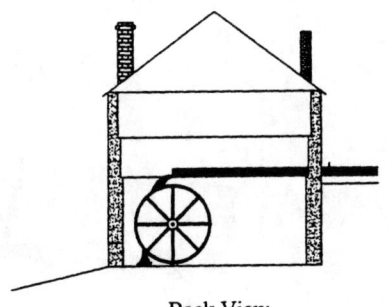

Back View

0   10   20   30   40   50

Drawings by: G. Kevin Steele

Front façade, c1928, showing sack hoist and hood, since removed.
(Courtesy of Iroquois Hunt Club)

North façade, c1928, with a view of the rear (east) wall.
(Courtesy of Iroquois Hunt Club)

Aerial view of the mill, c1928, showing the millrace and sluice. (Courtesy of Iroquois Hunt Club)

The wide, low dam (now gone) just upstream from the highway bridge. (Courtesy of Iroquois Hunt Club)

Grimes House, c1923.
(Charles Richardson, *The Building Stones of Kentucky*)

Aerial view of the mill, from a souvenir program for the Hunt Club, 1928, showing the Grimes House and the flax mill at the top of the hill. (Courtesy of University of Kentucky)

West (front) façade.

North façade.

South façade, with porch addition.

King-post truss in the attic.

East (rear) façade.

Stone types: Kentucky River Marble—large, smooth blocks;
Tyrone Limestone—smaller, rough-surfaced blocks.

16 ½ foot Fitz overshot water wheel.

Remnant of the dam abutment on the north bank of Boone Creek.

Stone-lined millrace at the dam,
showing the opening for the head gate.

One of the 39-inch diameter conglomerate millstones
at the mill entrance.

Pen and ink, Frances L. Smith, 1928.
(Courtesy University of Kentucky)

Pen and ink, Howard E. Smith, 1934.
(Courtesy Iroquois Hunt Club)

Kentucky River Marble is used predominantly in the mill's foundation blocks and is mixed with Tyrone Limestone in the courses of the first story. The blocks in the second story are mostly Tyrone. Generally speaking, the blocks of Kentucky River Marble used in the mill are much larger than the blocks of Tyrone Limestone.

The builders did not have to go far for the stone. Kentucky River Marble is exposed in ledges in front of the mill, at an elevation of about 670 feet above sea level. These ledges follow the contour of the hill through an area referred to at one time as the "quarry." The Kentucky River Marble used in the mill was probably taken from this quarry, as well as from ledges directly in front of the mill. Tyrone Limestone is exposed at higher elevations, starting at about 700 feet above sea level. There is a small quarry in this formation located only 200 yards from the mill on north side of Grimes Mill Road. This quarry is large enough to have supplied all of the Tyrone Limestone used in the mill construction. The quarry had the added advantage of a downhill route all the way to the mill site.[6]

Some of the surrounding ledge had to be removed at the mill site to provide a solid, level foundation for the basement stone. The basement is all below grade at the front of the mill (west façade). The site slopes down toward the creek, and the outside basement wall at the back of the mill (east façade) is all above grade. The east end of the basement—the wheel pit—is excavated to a greater depth than the other two-thirds in order to accommodate the water wheel. The wheel pit is about 12 feet by 36 feet and over 16 feet deep. Approximately one-third of the basement (the front or west end) has a modern poured-concrete floor, and the middle one-third is unfinished. The floor in the wheel pit could not be observed, as it is covered by several feet of standing water. There is a small stone arch, near the floor on the south wall, that directed water from the wheel pit to the tailrace (now filled in).

The walls vary regularly in thickness—3 feet in the basement, 2 ½ feet in the first story, and 2 feet in the second story. The horizontal courses vary in height, decreasing from about 12 inches high in the basement to about 6 inches high in the second story. The stone dimension also decreases as it courses up; basement blocks vary in width from about 1 to 5 feet, and the second-story blocks from about 6 to 30 inches. There is a north-south interior basement wall, 2 feet thick, separating the main basement from the water wheel pit.

It appears that there were originally six door openings in the mill. All are roughly 4 feet wide by 6 ½ feet high. One basement door on the east façade provides entry to the wheel pit. There were two matching doors on this wall at one time, but one has been filled in with stone. There is a walk-out basement door from the south façade that now leads into the basement below the enclosed porch. The 20-foot by 50-foot porch is a modern addition, installed by the Iroquois Hunt Club in 1962.[7] The south basement wall has been partially covered with fill. The porch and associated fill hide the original basement door, several windows, and the archway at the base of the wheel pit. The south wall is pictured in a photograph and two sketches of the mill made prior to addition of the porch.[8]

There are three doors on the west (front) façade, providing a main entrance on the first floor and loading access from the second floor and attic. The three doors are vertically aligned. Above the doors, a beam projected out from the ridge of the gable. The protruding beam and hood appears in a 1929 photograph but was subsequently removed. It would have anchored a pulley used for hoisting loads up and down from the second floor and attic.

The best estimate of the number of original window openings is twenty-five. All window penetrations are in stone, except for those in the frame attic—two in the west gable and two that were formerly in the east gable. One former window in the south wall of the first floor has been enlarged to make a new doorway into the enclosed porch addition. Although window sizes vary, most are roughly 3 feet wide and 50 to 60 inches high. Pegged wood window frames, made from 5-inch by 7-inch timbers, are very old. Most sashes have 12 panes, 6 over 6, and appear to be early twentieth century.

Two chimneys penetrate the roof. The smaller of the pair, about 28 inches by 24 inches, is located on the north side, its base resting on the north-south interior wall that separates the main basement from the wheel pit. This chimney, which is possibly an addition, does not serve a fireplace. It has round openings on the first floor and second floor to receive the metal flue from a coal or wood stove.

The large chimney serves a corner fireplace on the first floor. The stone chimney face is almost 11 feet wide. The fireplace opening is 4 ½ feet wide and 4 feet high. This area may have been partitioned to serve as the miller's office, a typical practice at the time.[9] There is also a fireplace opening in the basement—about 5 feet across by 3 feet high—that has a finely laid stone arch. There is no fireplace opening on the second floor.

Another unusual feature in the stonework is an arched opening in the north façade where the millrace ended. A wooden sluice, now gone, carried water from the millrace through the archway and over to the water wheel. The archway is 7 feet wide and 6 feet high. The opening in the stone wall would have accommodated a sluice 4 feet wide. The unsupported arch consists of fifteen tapered stones.

A smaller archway in the south façade at the base of the wheel pit, where water exited to the tailrace, has been buried under fill. The arch stones are visible from inside the wheel pit.

The stonework is in excellent condition. The exterior walls are still very close to true, and there are only minor, insignificant cracks in the stone. There is a noticeable concave curvature of the north wall, but it appears to be by design. The only noticeable structural defect is the large stone chimney, which is leaning slightly toward the roof ridge. The west end of the basement, being below grade, may have had problems with water seepage in the past. The stone joints in this area of the foundation have been remortared with a dark-colored, possibly waterproof, material that does not match the other mortar.

The wood framing of the mill consists of horizontal beams and joists supported by upright posts, all assembled with pegged mortise-and-tenon joints.[10] There is no evidence that any metal spikes, nails, bolts, or screws were used in construction of the framing. The main structural members consist of 12-inch by 12-inch timbers.[11] The first- and second-story floors rest on parallel 39-foot beams (two per floor) that start at the west wall and run west to east. Chop marks indicate that these are hand-hewn beams. These major beams are supported by four central posts per floor. A portion of each square post has been hewn to an octagonal-shaped column, one of the few decorative features found in the mill. The major beams are mortised to accept tenons from the upright columns. The four basement posts have been supplemented by a number of steel support posts.

The joists for the first- and second-story floors are 4-inch by 9-inch timbers that run north-south on spacing that varies from about 24 to 30 inches on center. The major floor beams are mortised to accept the joist tenons, and each joint is held in place with a peg.

The attic floor is supported by two parallel 39-foot beams that run north-south from wall to wall. The beams are supported by four central posts, similar to the ones on the floor below. Parallel beam sections running east-west from wall to wall are connected to the north-south beams by pegged mortise-and-tenon joints. Joists run north-south, the same as the floors below.

Flooring is tongue-and-groove poplar and pine planking, all twentieth century. The Iroquois Hunt Club installed a floor over the wheel pit on the east end of the first floor to accommodate a modern kitchen. It is uncertain how the wheel pit was separated from the first floor when originally constructed. The wall and floor in this area, if any were present, have been removed. All stairs and room partitions are modern additions. If there were any original partitions, none remain. Floor beams, joists, and posts bear evidence of considerable reworking of interior spaces in the past.

The mill has a pitched roof with a single gable, the ridge running east-west. The simple exterior belies a complex underlying structural system quite different from modern roofs.[12] The major support system is provided by two king-post trusses. These two massive central posts under the ridge each support sloping beams ("principal rafters"), which are braced with timbers connected to the posts. Much smaller "common rafters" run parallel to the principal rafters and are connected at the ridge by pegged mortise-and-tenon joints. There is no ridgepole. About half way down the roof slope on each side, horizontal beams, called "purlins," run from gable to gable. These beams are supported by 2-inch by 10-inch uprights that appear to be modern and may have been added during a roof repair project. The roof is covered with composition shingles supported by modern sheathing. The original shingles would have been made of wood.

There are two upright posts in the attic that have no function in the roof system. These were probably supports for some of the mill machinery. Holes bored in the posts indicate that they may have accommodated a horizontal shaft. The attic level would have had a number of shafts and pulleys for elevators, cleaners, hoists, and other features of an early nineteenth-century mechanized mill.

On the whole, the wood structure is in excellent condition. The roof ridge is slightly bowed in the center. The first- and second-story floors have experienced some sagging, which has been shored up at various times. There is some evidence of structural damage that has been repaired. Although largely intact, the roof has been worked on at different times. Besides the roof, the basement is the only other area where evidence of major repairs is obvious. A number of joists on the south end have been replaced with a combination of dimension lumber and cedar beams. Also in the basement, approximately the first 12 feet of the two major overhead beams have been cut out and replaced with new timbers. These rather drastic alterations may have been necessitated by water damage (see above) and subsequent decay, although other causes such as dry rot, termites, or fire cannot be ruled out. There is evidence of termite damage to other structural members in the basement.

Very little of the mill machinery is still in place. There is a steel water wheel in the wheel pit. The rims, spokes, and cross-members are all in good condition, but the buckets are rusting and badly deteriorated. The wheel was manufactured by the Fitz Water Wheel Company of Hanover, Pennsylvania. It is approximately 16 ½ feet in diameter and 44 inches wide and has 48 buckets. The wheel is mounted on an 18-foot long, 5-inch diameter steel axle, whose ends rest on heavily worn bearings. Fitz "steel overshoot water wheels" were shipped in "knocked down" sections that were assembled on site.[13] These sections had to fit through the doors into the wheel pit. Although the date of installation is unknown, steel wheels had become fairly commonplace by the turn of the century. They were more efficient and durable than wooden wheels, which warped and rotted and had to be replaced frequently.

No other mill-related machinery remains in place. The pair of millstones that decorate the front of the mill may be original.

> The old mill had two sets of the finest burrs in the country. These grinding stones are now part of the attractive entrance to the mill....[14]

In photographs from the 1950s, three stones may be seen, including a banded millstone that was no doubt one of the French buhrs. At some point, the metal bands may have rusted away and the segmented millstone separated into numerous pieces. The two 39-inch millstones that remain are made of conglomerate. Similar stones were made in Kentucky, as nearby as the Red River Millstone Quarry near Pilot Knob.[15]

Considerable modern equipment has been installed by the Hunt Club, including electrical wiring and plumbing, a furnace, air conditioning, a kitchen, and restrooms.

In 1870, Grimes Mill was using a 15-foot water wheel that produced 20 horsepower and powered two pairs of millstones.[16] We can speculate on some of the mill's other essential equipment and its location. Most of the power train would have been on the basement level. Because of their weight, the millstones probably would have been located on the first floor. Some means had to be provided to lift the runner stone up and turn it over on its back. The furrows in the stones required frequent sharpening to maintain a good grinding surface. The hoist could have been supported by the overhead beams on the first floor.

There would have been a cleaning machine to separate the chaff from the wheat before grinding. After grinding, the flour would have been sent to bolting chests for sifting into various grades of fineness. The finished product would have been directed to flour bins prior to loading into barrels. Flour barrels were stored on the first and second floors, where space was available. As a rule, the attic and basement were not used for storage due to heat and dampness, the two major enemies of flour. The old photograph shows the hood for the hoist pulley used to load the barrels into wagons. The pulley rope was probably attached to a windlass inside the mill that would have been water powered. Finally, merchant mills always had to have a good set of scales to weigh the flour barrels. Numerous other mechanical items may have been employed at Grimes Mill, but no evidence is available to substantiate their use.[17]

Since one person was reportedly able to operate the facility, the mill may have been designed along the lines of Oliver Evans' widely adopted plans for an "automated gristmill." Evans' patented equipment included (1) the elevator—a belt with buckets used to move grain vertically in a mill, for example to carry wheat and corn from the first floor to hoppers on the floors above, (2) the conveyor—an auger used to move grain horizontally in a mill, for example to deliver cleaned grain to the millstones for grinding, and (3) the hopper boy—a tub with a turning rake that cooled and dried the flour so it would not stick to the bolting screens.[18]

Grimes Mill Neighborhood
Roads 1808-1809

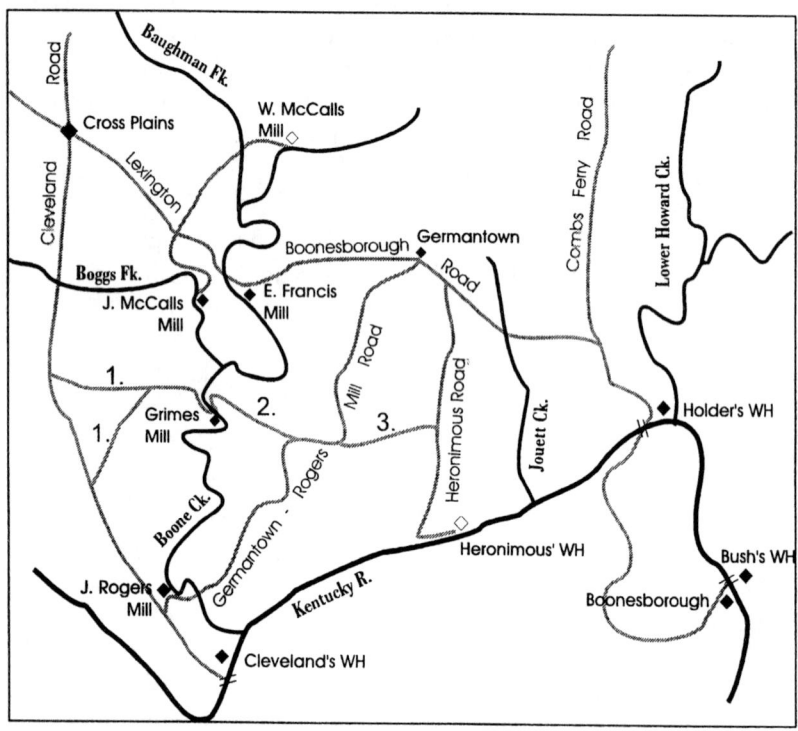

Placement of these roads is based on information in county road orders and Luke Munsell's 1818 map of Kentucky. Precise locations remain somewhat speculative. The sites of William McCall's mill and Heronimous' WH (warehouse) are only generally known. Ferries are shown as //.

Charles Grimes' roads:

1. From "Cleaveland road by the stone meeting House to the mill of Charles Grimes" and from "the same road [Cleveland] near to William Cottons to said Grimes mill."

2. From "the ford of Boons Creek opposite Charles Grimes Mill to where it will intersect Rogers road leading from German Town to Rogers Mill."

3. From "Grimes Mill Road where it intersects Rogers Road from thence to intersect Heronimous Road . . . where it goes down the Hill to Heronimous ware house."

Chapter 4

Early Years
1807-1837

S cant records are available for Grimes Mill during this period, but sufficient information is available to piece together a general picture of Charles Grimes' business activities. We know from numerous records that the mill was producing flour for sale during the period. There is extensive documentation of Charles' efforts to get new roads established to his mill. These roads were instrumental for transporting his flour to warehouses from where it could be shipped on the Kentucky River to markets downstream.

New Roads

Since wagons had to haul wheat in and flour out, Charles Grimes needed roads to make his gristmill a success. There is no evidence of a public road in this location prior to the mill's construction. In 1808, Charles asked the Fayette circuit court to open a "New Road" to his mill. He actually requested two short segments, each of which would run less than two miles to Cleveland Road. The first went

> from Cleaveland road by the stone meeting House
> to the mill of said Charles Grimes

and the second

> from the same road [Cleveland] near to William
> Cottons to said Grimes mill.[1]

Four commissioners were appointed "to view the ground on which a new road is proposed" and report to the court "the conveniences and inconveniences that will result as well to Individuals as the publick if said roads should be opened."

The proposed roads crossed land belonging to Eli Cleveland and John Poindexter. Poindexter objected, so the court then had to appoint a jury to view the property and assess damages. The jury returned its report in October, and the court ordered Grimes Mill Road "be opened & established at said Grimes expense." Charles Grimes was appointed overseer.[2]

The exact route of these roads is not apparent today. One may have followed present-day Grimes Mill Road between Boone Creek and Richmond Road, and the other may have veered off to the northwest toward Athens. The new roads not only allowed Fayette County wheat to reach Grimes Mill but also provided Charles a route to get his flour to Cleveland's warehouse on the Kentucky River.

Three months after he requested a new road in Fayette County, Charles petitioned the Clark County court to open a road

> from the ford of Boons Creek opposite Charles Grimes Mill to where it will intersect Rogers road leading from German Town to Rogers Mill.[3]

The commissioners returned a favorable report, and the court ordered the road established.[4]

Germantown has vanished but was once situated near the intersection of the Athens-Boonesboro Road and Jones Nursery Road. Portions of the old Germantown-Rogers Mill Road may still exist. Just south of Germantown, the road generally followed the course of what is today the Grimes Mill Road, the north-south section between Locust Grove and Munch's Corner. The Germantown-Rogers Mill Road then veered off to the south in the direction of Boone Ridge Lane. The final approach to Rogers Mill is gone now. Here the road had to descend a steep hill to Boone Creek.[5]

By this new road, Grimes was able to get his flour down to Rogers Mill. Building a road from one mill to another may seem odd at first, but there was a good reason for it. Charles was seeking another access point to get his flour on the river, and this was available from Rogers Mill. Clark Countians must have established the road in order to provide wagon access to Cleveland's warehouse, presumably via a ford downstream from Rogers' milldam.

In 1809, Charles Grimes requested yet another road from his mill, this one to run in Clark County

> from Grimes Mill Road where it intersects Rogers Road from thence to intersect Heronimous Road... where it goes down the Hill to Heronimous ware house.[6]

Heronimous Road was a north-south route between Germantown and the Kentucky River. Heronimous' warehouse, established the previous year, was located on the north side of the river, a little downstream from the mouth of Jouett Creek.[7] Evidently, Grimes was seeking an alternative to doing business at Cleveland's warehouse.

Merchant Mill

Gristmills in pioneer Kentucky generally were divided into two classes, custom mills and merchant mills. While he may have done some custom milling for his neighbors, Charles Grimes built his establishment as a merchant mill with his eye on a market far south of Kentucky.

Custom mills were designed to provide a service for nearby farmers, namely, grinding corn and wheat for their personal use. The miller's profit was the toll of corn meal or flour that he kept. These mills were the most common types in rural areas, where they reduced the farmer's labor to provide bread for his table.

Merchant mills were typically larger and more costly affairs with much greater profit potential. They were built along the lines of conventional manufacturing facilities, using raw materials to turn out a marketable product. Most merchant mills at that time were designed to grind wheat in quantity to produce flour by the barrel. Profitable operation required a large supply of available grain, a sizeable market for the flour, and efficient transportation routes to move each to and from the mill. The owner was likely to hire not only a miller to grind his grain but also coopers to make his barrels and wagoners to haul his product.

The emerging importance of merchant mills and the export market at the end of the eighteenth century led the Kentucky General Assembly to enact laws to regulate this enterprise. These acts established a series of warehouses, where "all boulted [sifted] wheat flour and every cask [barrel] thereof brought for exportation" could be inspected. Inspectors were appointed by the governor. Dimensions of barrels were specified in great detail, and the miller was to brand each one with his name and the tare and net weights. Each barrel was to contain 196 pounds of flour. The grade of flour—superfine, fine, or condemned—was to be branded on the barrel by the inspector. Any flour remaining in a warehouse for more than nine months was to be sold at public auction. It was unlawful to export any flour not inspected, to export "condemned" flour, or to alter a brand. This system of warehouses and inspectors was designed to discourage a fairly obvious list of unscrupulous practices. It was meant to help Kentucky's merchant mills compete in the growing export market by forcing manufacturers to supply a uniform commodity.[8]

Charles Grimes' road-building activity makes it apparent that he deemed access to the Kentucky River necessary for his mill to flourish. Combined with other evidence, it leads to the conclusion that Grimes Mill was intended from the outset to operate as a merchant mill. This helps explain why Charles put up a two-and-a-half-story stone building for his mill. Such a substantial structure was surely too costly to have been profitable grinding corn solely for local farmers.

Evidence suggests that most of the mills erected in the lower Boone Creek area in this period were the merchant type. Eli Cleveland's was a merchant mill, as he advertised in the *Kentucky Gazette*:

> Boats may come up from the river to the mills in
> high water. The whole beautifully situated for
> merchant business, at the mouth of Boon's creek.[9]

Evan Francis' (formerly Charles Hazelrigg's) mill complex on Boone Creek in Clark County featured "merchant grist and saw mills and distillery."[10] John McCall solicited wheat for his merchant mill through the *Gazette*:

> My Mill Is now in complete order for
> manufacturing of Flour, having a Shelling Mill, by
> which the first of the weavel is extracted from the
> grain, with the assistance of the Screen and Fan.
> Also a first rate pair of French Burrs. I wish to

purchase two or three thousand bushels of Wheat.
John M'Call, Near the Cross Plains.[11]

French burrs, or buhrs, were imported millstones made from high-
quality flint. Grimes Mill may have been similar in many respects
to John McCall's Mill, though the owner of the former chose not to
advertise in the *Gazette*. The location of these mills suggests that
they were looking at a far more lucrative market than Lexington. In
fact, Grimes and others intended to take advantage of the then
booming New Orleans market.

Kentucky was effectively separated from the eastern states by
the Allegheny Mountains. Because the roads were poor and the
distances long, the Commonwealth's agricultural and manufactured
products could not be gotten to these markets economically. At that
time, the only feasible transportation routes to distant markets were
rivers. Goods could be put on the Kentucky River and floated to the
Ohio. From there, the Ohio and Mississippi rivers formed a long,
navigable highway, at the end of which lay New Orleans,
eighteenth-century metropolis and port city.[12]

Numerous warehouses sprang up along the Kentucky River to
take in produce prior to loading on the river. Cleveland's
warehouse at Cleveland's Landing was closest to the Boone Creek
mills. Other warehouses nearby were William Bush's across from
Boonesborough, John Holder's at the mouth of Lower Howard
Creek, and Henry Heronimous' below the mouth of Jouett Creek, all
in Clark County. On the other side of the river, there was Stone's
warehouse at Stone's Ferry and the Jacks Creek warehouse at the
mouth of Jacks Creek, both on Green Clay's land in Madison
County.[13] Along with the warehouses, builders began constructing
flatboats to carry goods to New Orleans.[14] Eli Cleveland had a
boatyard at Cleveland's Landing. John Holder established one near
the mouth of Lower Howard Creek. Other individuals listed boats
for sale in the *Gazette*. In fact, the Grimes family may have been in
the boat business. Charles' brother, Benjamin Grimes, advertised a
boat for sale in 1802.[15]

Trade began in earnest with General James Wilkinson's
successful expedition to New Orleans in 1787. By the time it fell
into American hands following the Louisiana Purchase and

subsequent treaty with Spain, the city had become the major destination for Kentucky exported goods and produce—tobacco, pork, beef, hemp, *and flour*. The *Gazette* reported that in the first six months of 1802, Kentucky shipped over 85,000 barrels of flour to New Orleans.[16] Charles Grimes intended to take advantage of this booming market.

In the early 1800s, it was not clear to Kentucky citizens that the Mississippi River could be kept open for commerce or that New Orleans would continue to welcome it. After enduring Burr's Conspiracy, westerners faced the threat of losing New Orleans to Britain until the matter was finally settled by the War of 1812. Kentuckians volunteered for the war in great numbers, the Grimes family being no exception. Charles' son John may have been the John Grimes in Captain Richard Bledsoe's Fayette County rifle company who was captured in the defeat at River Raisin on January 22, 1813.[17]

Following the war, New Orleans continued to be the principal outlet for Kentucky's goods for many years to come. Charles Grimes rode his vision to wealth and prosperity. His business managed to succeed in a region teeming with mills.

Mills of Boone Creek

By the time Grimes Mill went into operation, there were numerous gristmills in the Boone Creek watershed, some of which had been established for many years. Charles Morgan had a mill on the east side of Boone Creek by 1784. This pioneer mill was shown on John Filson's map of Kentucky and was cited a number of times in the *Kentucky Gazette*. It was probably located on Morgan's 1,300-acre grant, which straddled the creek in Fayette and Clark counties. Fayette County order books refer to Charles Morgan's Mill on a road leading to Winchester. The mill may have been a little south of where present-day Sulphur Well Road ends at the creek.[18]

A little farther north on Boone Creek, Colonel William Robinson built a gristmill near "the joining of the middle, north and east forks." Robinson received approval from the court for a dam 5 feet high on the middle fork and a dam of 5 feet 3 inches high on the east fork.[19]

On the Fayette side, John McCall had a mill on Boone Creek about 11 miles east of Lexington at the Sulphur Well, which he later renamed "Harrogate." He also operated mills "near the Cross Plains" on the waters of Boone Creek, at a place he called the "Oak Ridge" on Boggs Fork. Here John established a merchant gristmill for the manufacture of wheat flour, plus a sawmill and a distillery.[20]

Another establishment in Clark County was Hazelrigg's Mills on Boone Creek. Hazelrigg died in 1796, and the business was subsequently operated by Evan Francis. The site included a merchant gristmill, sawmill, and distillery. The milldam was located about one-quarter of a mile downstream from where the Athens-Boonesboro Road crosses Boone Creek.[21]

James Beatty applied for permission to erect a mill on Boone Creek opposite the mouth of Boggs Fork, but upon receiving the jury's report, the court refused to establish his mill seat. It is not known if Beatty ever got his mill built.[22]

John McCall's brother, William McCall, had a gristmill and sawmill on Boone Creek, "one mile from the Cross-Plains." William later opened a fulling mill at this site.[23]

Eli Cleveland had a large mill complex—gristmill, sawmill, and hemp mill—near the mouth of Boone Creek. His mills burned in 1796, the work of arsonists, and that summer he put his whole enterprise up for sale. Jeremiah and Joseph Rogers acquired Cleveland's gristmill, which later became known as Rogers Mill. The gristmill and a later distillery operated into the Civil War years. The mill foundation and old road down to the creek are still visible.[24]

In addition to John McCall's, there were two other mills on Boggs Fork—John Winn Jr.'s mill about a mile southwest of Athens and the mill that Charles Grimes' advertised for sale in 1804. The latter mill may be the one referred to in a deed of sale from David Bibb's heirs to Charles Grimes. One of the property corners was "a old white Oak in the mill dam" on Boggs Fork.[25] Perrin's history mentions a fourth mill on Boggs Fork built by Owen Winn that "burned about fifteen years ago, and Pettitt's distillery stands [1882] near the same place."[26]

Two mills were located on Baughman Fork—Samuel Duncan's gristmill and sawmill "at John Frank's old mill" and William Christian's water gristmill.[27] George Sharp operated a mill near

Athens, which would have been on the "waters of Baughman Fork."[28]

The most intriguing gristmill from an historical perspective is the one often referred to as Pettit's Mill, but known also as Morton's Mill and Gentry's Old Mill. The building is still standing near the creek, just north of the road at the Athens-Boonesboro Road bridge and is now the site of the Bluegrass Christian Camp. The mill is beautifully constructed of Tyrone Limestone. In an early photograph (c.1919) taken before any modern additions were made, it bears a striking resemblance to Grimes Mill and may have been erected in the same timeframe. It lasted longer that any other mill on Boone Creek, except Grimes Mill. Although the mill is located on property that once belonged to Charles Hazelrigg, the builder has not yet been established.[29]

Although competition must have been lively with so many gristmills, Charles Grimes was able to turn his establishment into a profitable and long-lived concern. Of all those named above, none would outlast Grimes Mill.

A Man of Property

Charles Grimes was in the land business. His profits dealing in this commodity may have provided the capital to invest in his milling venture. Before 1800, we find Charles selling Kentucky land to his former neighbors back in Virginia. A few years later, he advertised land and mills for sale in the *Kentucky Gazette*.[30]

The first record of Charles purchasing land in Fayette County was his acquisition of 45 acres adjoining his father's plantation on Baughman Fork.[31] By 1810, Charles owned 180 acres on Baughman Fork and 100 acres on Boone Creek.

Several of Charles' transactions involved the Winn family. He bought a farm near Athens from Lettice Winn. Lettice, the widow of George Winn, lost several lawsuits involving land claims in Clark County, and in order to pay the judgements, the Winn family seat was sold at auction.[32]

Charles acquired another tract near Athens, one on which Daniel Boone had established his settlement. He bought the parcel "known as Boons Station" from Lettice Winn's son-in-law, John Hendley. Charles paid Hendley "362 Barrells of Superfine flower."[33]

Charles added to his holdings on Boone Creek, buying up farms adjoining the mill tract to increase the size of his plantation. The most significant purchase was 155 acres on Boone Creek, north of the mill, which he obtained from the heirs of David Bibb. This land was bounded by Boggs Fork and McCalls Mill Road.[34] Charles probably obtained this and other Boone Creek properties for raising crops—wheat, cotton, corn, rye, and barley—to feed his gristmill and for harvesting timber to feed his sawmill.

Charles bought other property in the area,[35] and one of these involved him in a string of lawsuits. Land titles in Kentucky were the bane not only of the original settlers, but also their children and, in some cases, their grandchildren. The problem affected everyone, rich or poor. Phillip Grimes lost sizeable portions of his two land grants from the state of Virginia, both on Stoner Creek. Charles was very careful—or lucky—in his land dealings, and had not lost any property due to conflicting claims. That changed in 1810, when Charles contracted to buy 51 acres on Boggs Fork from James Graves. James, who lived in Orange County, Virginia, inherited the land from his father, Richard Graves, who had lived in the Boone Creek neighborhood. Charles signed a bond for $540 to pay for the property, and Graves signed a penalty bond of $1,000 to be paid Charles if Graves could not provide "a good and sufficient deed." Grimes did not pay his bond by the due date, since the title to part of the tract was being contested by others. The issues raised in the suit were complex and demand lengthy explanation. It boiled down to a simple matter for Grimes—he claimed that Graves could not make "a good & sufficient" deed for the property.[36]

The first problem was that Richard Graves' widow took her dower out of the 51 acres. To replace this loss, James Graves laid off another 12 acres to include in Grimes' deed. Unfortunately, according to the surveyor, William Cotton, the new parcel interfered with William Gillespie's patent. In spite of these problems for the buyer, Graves and his Fayette County agent, John Price, repeatedly sued Grimes for payment. In 1817, Grimes turned the tables and sued Graves, arguing that he had "long since paid the purchase money." Grimes complained that

he has not only been kept out of the possession &
enjoyment of said tract of land & lost the rents of
the Same, but hath sustained other injuries by
means of timber, rails &c removed therefrom to a
considerable amount.[37]

Apparently, none of these suits satisfactorily resolved the issue of
whether Grimes had paid the "purchase money" or whether Graves
had given him "a good & sufficient" deed. Two years later, Graves
was back in court complaining that Grimes had cut down a large
quantity of timber on the land.

Charles Grimes' other purchases included a tract on Panther
Creek in Ohio County and three lots in Winchester, one with a
frame house, one a brick house, and one a brick stable.[38]   One of
these lots belonged to Henry C. Clay, Grimes' son-in-law. Clay got
into financial trouble and had to put up his house and lot in
Winchester to secure one of his debts. When he could not pay what
he owed, his home was sold at public auction, and "the said Lott
was set up to the highest bidder and cryed off to Charles Grimes of
the county of Fayette."[39]

Clay must have been in desperate straits. At about the time he
was being sued in Clark County, Clay was suing his father-in-law in
Fayette County for $6,000. Clay complained that Charles Grimes
owed him

- $3,000 for a loan,
- $2,000 "reasonably due" Clay for work performed for
  Grimes, including "with the servants, oxen, carts, horses
  and waggons of [Clay], making and repairing fences on the
  land of [Grimes] and building and refining divers houses on
  the same land."
- $750 for "divers quantities of hemp delivered at his
  [Grimes'] request," and
- $250 for miscellaneous other debts.[40]

The documents filed with this case do not indicate how the matter
was finally resolved. It seems unlikely, however, that Clay got his
$6,000.

One could not be faulted for forming the impression that early Kentuckians spent a lot of energy suing each other and that many people had financial problems. The two phenomena were often closely related. In the West, as Kentucky was known at that time, cash money was hard to come by—there was simply too little in circulation. The inhabitants managed to get along in a barter economy, but for large transactions they often had to resort to "paper"—bonds, notes, etc. If you were holding a note on someone for $1,000, you might give another party your note for $1,000 to buy, say, 100 acres of land. You might have to go to court to try to collect your $1,000, and if you could not recover it, you would end up in court and lose the land that you had "bought." This was a fairly common scenario that had many complicated variations. For every person who ended up in court because he was too ornery to pay his debts, another was there because of circumstances largely beyond his control.

By 1819, when his land holdings leveled off, Charles owned over 2,000 acres in Kentucky. While he bought much more than he sold, Grimes did occasionally let a piece of property go. In 1816, ten years after his father died, Charles sold the old homeplace to Benjamin Harrison. The tract was part of the survey patented to Robert Boggs, purchased by Phillip Grimes, and inherited by Charles Grimes.[41]

Grimes Quarry

Since Charles Grimes built his mill and house from locally quarried limestone, it is not surprising to learn that he turned this resource into yet another business enterprise. Boone Creek cuts through some of Kentucky's oldest sedimentary rocks laid down nearly 500 million years ago in the Ordovician Period. Tapping into the limestone cliffs lining the creek, Charles opened what would become one of the most noted rock quarries in the state. High-quality building stone was mined for use in construction projects as far away as Frankfort. Two formations of the High Bridge Group of limestone and dolomite were worked for their superior properties:

> *Tyrone*—"Birdseye limestone." Dense, grey, dove, or cream-colored limestone, breaking with conchoidal fracture, and with small facets of coarsely crystalline calcite. On weathering the

surface becomes white, in which the darker facets
are conspicuous, giving rise to the name Birdseye.

Oregon—"Kentucky River Marble." Grey to cream
and buff-colored, granular, magnesian limestone. It
is barren of fossils.[42]

The Oregon Formation varies from 30 to 65 feet thick and the
Tyrone up to 90 feet thick. Kentucky River Marble was known in
earlier times as "Grimes building stone." Stone from Charles
Grimes' quarry was used for the columns of the Old Capitol in
Frankfort. The quarry would later supply the stone for the Henry
Clay monument in Lexington cemetery and for the Daniel Boone
monument in Frankfort cemetery.[43] The local newspaper mentioned
the quarry in a story about the Clay monument:

> Native magnesian limestone, found best for the
> monument in tests conducted by Dr. Robert Peter,
> was quarried in solid blocks, without seam, joint or
> fracture, of immense proportion at Grimes Quarry,
> near the present Grimes Mill, on Boone's Creek.[44]

The article stated that forty-two men "were engaged on the
monument and in the quarries."

There were several quarries on Charles' plantation. A small one
was located between the milldam and the mill, just below where the
kennels are today. The millrace flowed along the face of the quarry.
This fact was first mentioned in an early deed, which stated that the
race began "at the Mill dam running thence with the *stone quarry* to
the Mill road."[45] This quarry provided Kentucky River Marble for
construction of the mill and dam. Another quarry, this one in the
Tyrone Limestone, also supplied stone for the mill and dam—and
possibly for the house. This quarry is about 100 feet north of
Grimes Mill Road, just down the hill from the Grimes House.
Finally, a large quarry in the Tyrone Limestone was located near the
top of a cliff, about one-third of a mile downstream from the
gristmill.

No occupations or businesses related to quarrying in the Boone
Creek area are found in the population or manufacturers censuses
from 1850 to 1870.[46] Quarrying work may have been too temporary
to be listed. It would have been even more sporadic in Charles'

time. No records exist to tell how involved Charles was in the process, but we know he was engaged in quarrying over a long period of time, beginning with the construction of his stone gristmill, dam, and house. Whatever his arrangement with stonecutters, the limestone resource helped in some measure to advance Charles' growing wealth.

Other Business Interests

Charles Grimes' had other businesses that flourished during these early years. In addition to the gristmill and his land dealings, he opened a limestone quarry and oversaw a diverse agricultural enterprise. We know that he raised cattle and horses and grew wheat, corn, flax, and cotton and that he had a large number of slaves to help in these enterprises. He also raised hogs in quantity.[47] Raising hogs was frequently associated with milling, which provided a food source (bran) that otherwise would have been a waste product. Charles may have exported pork to New Orleans in addition to flour. In addition to milling and quarrying, Charles carried on other small-scale manufacturing at his cotton mill, flaxhouse, sawmill, and small distillery.

Charles Grimes had a cotton mill in the bottom land on the Clark County side of the creek, just upstream from the gristmill dam. The "factory" had its own dam. Charles leased the cotton mill to one James Minter. The lease included

> the lot & parcel of ground lying and being in the County of Clarke on Boon's creek, bounded by said Creek on one side and the hill on the other, as they meander, containing all the bottom ground extending from Grimes's mill dam to the new dam for the factory with all its appurtenances and improvements.[48]

Minter was to pay $150 a year in rent. Grimes later threw into the bargain a house, kitchen, and stable for an additional $45 a year. Minter got in arrears on his rent, and Grimes, fearing that Minter "would remove his effects out of [the] County" without paying, went to court and obtained an order to "attach and seize the good and chattels" of Minter. We get a good description of the mill's contents from the list of "goods and chattels."

> one Cotton carding Engine, one Roving Frame with apparatus, one Reel, one Single Throstle, one Double Throstle unfinished, one Turning Lath, one Vice, two Iron Shafts[49]

Some of these terms are no longer in use. A carding engine was a device fitted with rows of wire teeth, which was used to pull apart and disentangle cotton fibers. A roving frame pulled and twisted the fibers prior to spinning. And a throstle was a machine used to spin cotton fibers into thread or cord. From the reference to the "new dam," we may infer that the cotton mill was water powered, but other details are not available. When he died, Charles still had the cotton mill, which was listed in the inventory of his estate.[50]

The Grimes Mill complex includes a stone foundation, 23 feet by 32 feet, referred to as the remains of a flaxhouse. The stone ruins are located on the north side of Grimes Mill Road, opposite the Grimes House. Although this must have been a significant structure, it was not mentioned in early records. It was still standing in the twentieth century; the one-and-a-half story structure can be seen in a photograph in the Hunt Club's souvenir program dated May 1928.[51]

In their 1805 petition to the court, Winn and Grimes sought permission for a gristmill *and sawmill*. The sawmill was probably a small affair and, given its location, probably water powered. Its products would have had many uses in Grimes' other businesses— making staves for flour casks and whiskey barrels, for example. Any excess production could have been sold locally.

James Jenkins signed a contract to supply Charles Grimes with at least "one hundred & twenty bushels of Merchantable Wheat," for which Grimes was to pay him in "plank that will be suitable for the inside of a house." The contract stated that Jenkins had already received $26.50 worth of plank. When Jenkins failed to deliver any wheat, Grimes sued him for broken covenant.[52]

If the accusations of James Graves were accurate, Grimes may have been operating a substantial sawmill. Graves and Grimes were in court for years in a land dispute. In one of their suits, Graves claimed that in the month of January 1816, Grimes came on his land and "cut a large quantity of timber, towit"

> 500 oak trees, 500 ash trees, 500 cherry trees, 500 walnut trees, and 500 sugar, buckeye, [and] hackberry trees.[53]

Graves sought $1,000 for his losses. The jury ruled against Grimes but only assessed damages in the amount of one cent.

There are indications that Charles was in the whiskey business from early times. One reference to this activity comes from the "historical tradition."

> The toll for milling was one-eighth of flour or meal, and it was not long before Grimes had more than he could use, so he erected a malt house and a distillery and for years "Old Grimes' Whiskey" made at the rate of three barrels a day was as famous as the flour and meal.[54]

Charles Grimes probably operated a small distillery in conjunction with his mill, a fairly common association at that time. His neighbors John McCall, Evan Francis, and Jeremiah Rogers made whiskey at their mills. In 1810, the county could count 139 stills, so it might be a little surprising if Grimes did not have one.[55] The copy of an old receipt for whiskey supports this notion:

> Received of Charles Grimes four Barrels of whisky marked 42—33 ¾—33—30 ¾. Received by me at Cleavelands ware house for the youse of David Williamson. John Arvin 4th February 1814[56]

In the early 1800s, Eli Cleveland was a formidable presence in the Boone Creek area. Charles had a number of dealings with the notorious Cleveland, not all of which were pleasant. Their first recorded encounter, which resulted in the purchase of the mill tract on Boone Creek, was the most satisfactory one. Cleveland, apparently, was not well liked in the district. Arsonists burned his mills in 1796, and he took to the newspaper to excoriate his enemies. A clue as to why he was so disliked may be discerned from the deposition of John Bledsoe:

> I understood a man was in our neighborhood that had located on some of the land, and he thought he could take it away from everybody. This was Eli Cleveland.[57]

This deposition was made twenty years after the incident, so Cleveland's perfidy must have made a strong impression on Bledsoe. Eli could not get along with his own family. His brother Oliver stated that Eli bought a large quantity of land from their brother Alexander, but that "suit had to be brought for said money."[58]

Disagreement between Cleveland and Grimes began with a contract between Charles Grimes and Levi Hart. Hart was to deliver to Grimes

> at his Mill, for the purpose of being Manufactured, Wheat sufficient to make Eighty five Barrells of Flour, two thirds Superfine and one third fine... and deliver the Same in good Barrels, agreeably to Law, at Clevelands landing on the Bank of the Kentucky river, clear of all expence, inspection as well as otherwise.[59]

Grimes was to get "a certain bay horse" in payment, which he did receive. Subsequently, the deal fell through, and Hart sued for breach of contract. As it turned out, before an agreement could be signed, Hart came to Grimes and said that he and Cleveland wished to contract with Grimes for a larger quantity of flour, 350 to 400 barrels, to which Grimes agreed. Polly Clay, Grimes' daughter, explained what happened next:

> Mr. Hart observed that he would draw an article of agreement agreeable to their contract and bring it down as soon as convenient. And when Mr. Hart came down with the Article, he presented it to my father, and my father looked at said article and

> observed, Mr. Hart is this the contract, and Hart
> answered, No, it is not, But Mr. Cleveland dictated
> and I was obliged to write it so, and Mr. Hart
> observed that he told Mr. Cleveland at the drawing
> of said article that Mr. Grimes would not sign it,
> Because it was not the contract he had made with
> Mr. Grimes.[60]

Cleveland's scheme was to get Grimes to deliver all 400 barrels of
flour for the "agreed to" bay horse. Understandably, Grimes refused
to do any more grinding for the pair. The following exchange was
recorded in Polly Clay's deposition:

> Question by Charles Grimes. Did I not observe to
> Mr. Hart, when he brought the article above
> mentioned, that if he would write one agreeable to
> contract and bring it down, I would sign it.

> Answer. Yes you did, or words to that amount.[61]

The jury decided in Grimes' favor and allowed him "to recover his
costs herein expended."

Richard Spurr Jr. was serving as Charles Grimes' miller at this
time. In the papers filed with the suit, there are several receipts for
wheat received at the mill signed by Spurr. And in one of the
depositions, Charles Grimes asked if Mr. Hart had not agreed "that
Dicky Spurr must be the miller." "Dicky" was Richard Spurr Jr.,
whose brother James married Susanna Winn, daughter of Owen
Winn.[62]

From the above suit and others, we gain some insight into how
Charles Grimes' merchant milling business worked. We see him
producing flour for others to ship to market. While he may have
ventured into shipping as well, in many cases he was content to take
his profit at home and not hazard the risk of losing his investment
on the trip to New Orleans. The following suit brings out this point
and provides a sense of comic justice.

The Aubry brothers—Richard, Thomas, and Henry—stated in a
petition to Fayette circuit court that they had contracted with
Charles Grimes, "the owner of a merchant mill in the county," for

the manufacture of 200 barrels of flour, two-thirds superfine and one-third fine. Their petition stated that Grimes

> intending to practice a fraud upon your orators, did so brand the flour on the heads of the barrels, where in truth & in fact the flour was of a very inferior kind, so that when your orators had it carried to the port of New Orleans for market, they were forced to sell it at a much lower price than either fine or Superfine.[63]

In Grimes' answer, he denied that any of the flour was inferior and that the Aubrys had "called frequently at Defendants Mills to see said Flour... and declared themselves well satisfied and pleased." Grimes then turned to the heart of the matter:

> While said Flour was manufacturing, he [Grimes] required said complainants to have the same inspected before it was taken from Kentucky, which said complainants declined doing.[64]

In other words, the Aubrys had attended the production of their flour to ensure it was well made, and then tried to save a few dollars by not having the flour inspected—in violation of Kentucky law. Dudley Hudson "steered the boat to New Orleans in the Spring of 1817 for Richard and Thomas Aubry, loaded among other things with about two hundred and forty or fifty barrels of flour." The rest of the story is not hard to imagine. In New Orleans, when it was noted that the barrels did not bear the Kentucky inspector's brand, the locals proceeded to take advantage of the sellers' predicament. That the Aubrys had the nerve to come back home and sue Grimes showed additional misjudgment. The court ruled for Grimes.

Archibald Coleman was the miller at Grimes Mill during this time. In a deposition for the Aubry case, Coleman stated that

> when [I] began to Manufactor Flour in the year 1816 for Charles Grimes, said Grimes came into the Mill....

> Question by Charles Grimes. Have you not heard me say that it was my Wish always to make & deliver good Flour from my Mill.

Answer. I never thought you had any disposition to make or send away any Flour from your mill without it was good.[65]

Like his neighbors, Charles was in court often to defend against or collect debts. On balance, he probably came out well ahead. His losses never pushed him to the brink of insolvency. He was involved in one venture, however, with William Grimes Jr. that resulted in huge losses for both. William Leavy in his memoirs recalled William Grimes Jr.'s store: in Lexington:

> William W. Grimes who had acted for a year or more as Clerk for my father [William Leavy Sr.] opened a store on Main Street.[66]

Leavy did not provide the date, but it must have been about 1814, the year that William Grimes Jr. & Co. announced in the *Kentucky Gazette*:

> Have just received from Philadelphia an entire new assortment of Fresh Goods, which were purchased for cash at a most favorable time, just after the arrival of the "Bramble." Those who may wish to purchase will please call. Their assortment is composed of the most fashionable articles, suitable for the spring and summer seasons, which will be sold *cheap* for cash. They have opened in the *white house* opposite the market lately occupied by Stevens & Dallam.[67]

William's original partner in Grimes & Co. was William H. Tegarden, but that arrangement fell through less than a month after it began.[68] Another associate was Charles Grimes, who signed many of the notes William Jr. gave to buy merchandise for the store.

The company was still a going concern the following year, when William began advertising again in the *Gazette*. One of the notices gave additional information about his diversified business.

> New Goods. William Grimes, Jun'r. Has just received from the Eastward, and now opening, a large and general assortment of Dry Goods,

Groceries, Hardware, Queensware, Glassware, &c.
with a variety of Fall and Winter Fancy Goods of
the latest fashion, All of which he will sell
unusually low, Wholesale or Retail. Those having
open accounts, will please call and have them
adjusted.[69]

The last phrase was prophetic. William's business succeeded in
selling goods but did a poor job of collecting payment for them.
Many of his cash-strapped customers were allowed to buy on credit.
William placed a notice in the *Gazette* asking "those indebted to
him to settle their accounts."[70]   Such statements were common in
the newspaper and often meant that the creditors had begun to
demand payment. In William's case, the sharks were circling their
victim. In less than a year, he would be jailed for debt.

In the short time he was in business, William ran up staggering
debts, which he could not pay because his customers were not
paying him. In 1816, William committed all of his personal and
real property to trustees to sell in order to pay off as many of his
debts as possible.   A document accompanying this agreement
itemized the claims of thirty-seven creditors—totaling over
$30,000—and listed eight more creditors with open accounts,
amounts not specified.[71]

Charles Grimes had guaranteed several of William's notes. The
claims against Charles totaled nearly $10,000, including $1,000 to
John Hendley, $5,100 to the Bank of Kentucky, $787 to Neil &
Hurley, Merchants, in Philadelphia, and $2,400 to Lewis Lay &
Nicholas Thuron, Merchants.[72]   The latter merchants caused the
greatest problem for William Grimes.

In February of 1816, Lay & Thuron obtained a judgment against
William in Fayette circuit court for $1,236, "by virtue of which
William Grimes was duly committed to the Prison of the said
County in custody of Nathaniel Prentiss, Jailer."[73]   That month
William announced that the house in Lexington where he had his
store was "for rent," effectively signaling that he was out of
business.[74]   After getting out of jail, William spent the next few
years in court.   So did Charles, who experienced the costly and
distressing results of doing business with his unfortunate relative.[75]

Grimes House

Charles Grimes built a lavish stone mansion on the hill above Boone Creek. This house is a well-preserved historical landmark and is still referred to as the "Grimes House." The late Clay Lancaster called it "the finest stone house existing in Fayette County." He described some of its features in precise architectural terms:

> [The house] consists of a five-bayed, two storied principal mass, with a lower wing, also of two floors, at one end, and a low ell attached to the latter at right angles. The windows in the main block are tall, indicating high ceilings. The stonework is laid with exquisite care, especially the façade toward the stream, with alternating square and horizontal blocks reflecting the pattern of contemporary Flemish bond brickwork. The wood trim inside is finely detailed. In the parlor off the transverse stairhall the fireplace is flanked by shallow niches enframed by an archivolt springing from reeded pilasters, matching those of the mantel.[76]

The house is built of Tyrone Limestone in three sections. The two-and-a-half-story main structure with chimneys at both ends probably dates from 1813.[77] The home originally faced southeast, overlooking the mill, but the main entrance is now on the opposite (northwest) side. A lower two-story wing is attached at the southwest end. It may predate the main structure and could have been built about the same time as the mill. The one-story addition on the southeast side is of later construction; it was remodeled in 1980 to two stories.[78] The home must have been quite a showplace at the time it was built and gives some indication of the increasing affluence of Charles Grimes.

While residing in his new home, Charles continued accumulating properties in the Boone Creek area, and by 1819, at the height of his holdings, he was assessed for almost $30,000 worth of real estate and other taxable property, including 13 slaves and 6 horses.   Presumably, his milling activities made a significant contribution to his riches.

Passing the Torch

In his later years, old Grimes began distributing some of his property to his children.   His land holdings and taxable estate dropped to less than 1,400 acres and $18,000 in the years preceding his death.   His Boone Creek plantation was recorded as 511 acres.[79]

Charles Grimes died on August 8, 1837, at the age of sixty-six. He was laid to rest in the family burial ground on his plantation, near his sons John and Philip, who preceded him in death.   The cemetery, located about a hundred yards northwest of the house, is surrounded by a low wall of quarried stone.[80]

Charles wrote a detailed will, naming his wife Jane executrix and sons Charles William Grimes and Carlo Grimes executors.   To each of them, Charles left one-third of "my home residence and all of the lands pertaining thereto in Clark and Fayette Counties," which included the gristmill.[81]   His personal property included numerous pieces of fine furniture, a typical set of farm implements, and an ample supply of livestock.[82]

Chapter 5

Middle Years
1837-1887

G ood documentation is available for Grimes Mill after the Civil War, but records are scarce for the antebellum years. A rare early directory of Fayette County allows identification of the families living near the mill in 1838.[1] The landholders on "Boon's Creek road" included George Boone Jr., Mrs. Nancy Gentry, Sarah Graves, Mrs. Graves, Mrs. Jane Grimes and Son (Charles W.), Mrs. Rachael Grimes (widow of John Grimes), William Grimes, Cornelius Vaughan, and William Vaughan.

No significant community developed around Grimes Mill. Because Charles Grimes had accumulated such large holdings on Boone Creek, there were no stores or public facilities near the mill and very few neighbors. The only businesses located within the mill and farm complex were those operated by or in conjunction with the Grimes family.

When Charles died, he intended for his plantation and business ventures, including Grimes Mill, to be carried on by his two youngest sons, Charles W. and Carlo. At that time, Carlo was twenty-seven years old and his brother Charles W., who would become the dominant partner, was only twenty. They would face a number of challenges in trying to match their father's success.

Two outside events that occurred during this period had a profound effect on Grimes Mill and the Grimes family. The first was the Civil War. Charles W. Grimes was a slaveholder, and two of his sons went off to serve in the Confederate Army. At least one of their Fayette County relations—Lewis Grimes—fought on the Union side.[2] The unhappy consequences arising from divided loyalties affected many Bluegrass families. In addition to wartime inflation, Kentuckians suffered economically for their "neutrality," none more so than those identified as "lukewarm Unionists or Southern sympathizers."[3] The Civil War was the price the country had to pay to end slavery.

Near the end of the war, slaves in Kentucky could purchase their freedom by enlisting in the federal army. At least one of the Grimes slaves probably took advantage of this opportunity. The 1890 veterans census identified Charles W. Grimes, then living in Lexington, as a former private "who served in the Army, Navy, or Marine Corps of the United States during the war of the rebellion." The city directory for that year had a listing for

> Grimes, Charles W., colored, plasterer, residence 49
> Payne Street.[4]

All the remaining slaves in Kentucky were freed following ratification of the Thirteenth Amendment. At his death, Charles Grimes' will devised to his heirs twenty-one slaves plus their children. In 1860, Carlo owned six slaves, Charles W. owned twelve.[5] After the war, without slaves available to perform the physical labor associated with their varied enterprises, the Grimes family had to hire workers to accomplish these tasks.

But while the cultural landscape had been turned upside down, the greatest challenge for many following the war was economic. The other signal event for the Grimeses was the coming of the railroads, which displaced the Kentucky River as the main transportation artery from the Bluegrass region. Gristmills located near the river had an economic advantage in the days when the only route to markets beyond Kentucky was by water. As Dr. Thomas Clark so eloquently stated for Fayette's neighbor, "not one of the farm products of Clark County could pay its transportation costs overland, not even whiskey."[6] The first train from Louisville reached Lexington in 1851 and from Cincinnati in 1854.[7] As railways proliferated, locomotives replaced flatboats as the movers of Kentucky's commerce. Warehouses disappeared from the river, and manufacturing grew in Lexington at the expense of rural areas. Boone Creek, and specifically Grimes Mill, began to experience increasing isolation.

In a broader context, industry in Kentucky and the nation underwent an economically and socially significant transition, from farm-based industries to large-scale, urban-based industries. In addition to the production of crops and livestock, prosperous farms before the war usually carried on several small-scale manufacturing enterprises, such as spinning, weaving, carding and fulling, tanning, blacksmithing, woodworking, distilling, *and milling*. In the years after the war, the available labor pool began migrating to the cities, railroads were hauling raw materials in and finished products out, and coal- and wood-produced steam was supplanting water power as the preferred source of motive power. Business concerns were investing larger sums of money in ever-larger plants, whose operations were more efficient and whose products were cheaper. Many small industries would suffer, some would never recover. Gristmills were among their number.

At the outbreak of the Civil War, there was still a significant amount of industry in the Boone Creek area. There were two gristmills operating on Boone Creek in addition to Grimes Mill, one owned by J. E. Rogers and one by Sarah Pettit. There was a mill on Boggs Fork operated by R. Adams ("Fayette Mills") and three more, whose locations are uncertain, operated by James Halladay, David Stone, and Joe Carter. Halladay and Stone were each grinding corn, rye, and barley in proportions indicating that their output was destined for one of the area distilleries. Distilleries were operated by Adams and Rogers in Fayette and by Granville Smitha in Clark. Other industries included the sawmills of Levi Hart and Joe Carter and the blacksmith shop of wagonmaker Jacob Embry.[8]

At this time, the Grimes Mill complex still included a sawmill. It was shown on an 1861 map of Fayette County, on Boone Creek adjacent to the gristmill.[9] No reference to the sawmill after that date has been found.

Jane Grimes outlived her husband by nineteen years. She died on August 2, 1856, and was buried beside Charles Grimes in the family cemetery. At her death, Carlo and Charles W. Grimes became sole proprietors of the mill, as provided in their father's will.

Carlo Grimes

Carlo Grimes was born in Fayette County in 1810.[10] At that time, his father's mill was in operation, but the stone mansion house had not yet been completed. In 1835, Carlo was listed on the

Fayette County tax rolls with no property of his own. After their
father died, Carlo and his brother must have come to an agreement
on the homeplace, as Charles W. remained in Grimes House and
Carlo moved across the creek to Clark County.

Carlo married Maria Louisa Talbott of Bourbon County.[11] The
Grimes family had many ties to Bourbon, where several of Phillip's
children married or resided.   In the early nineteenth century,
Phillip's descendants could be found in the Athens-Boone Creek
area of Fayette, the Boone Creek area of Clark, and southern end of
Bourbon near the corner of Fayette and Clark.

There were several Grimes-Talbott family connections. Carlo's
sister, Mary "Polly," married Benjamin Talbott following the death
of her first husband. Two months after he married, Carlo purchased
from Polly and her husband a farm on the east side of Boone
Creek.[12] Carlo and his wife resided in Clark for over forty years,
raising all eight of their children there. For the census taker, Carlo
always stated that his occupation was farming. In 1860, the year
before the Civil War began, Carlo, age fifty, and Louisa, age forty-
two, lived in a household with their eight children, ranging in ages
from two to eighteen. Carlo lived up the hill from the gristmill, on
the south side of Grimes Mill Road.[13]

Grimes Mill was not listed among the manufacturing
establishments in Fayette County in 1860, but there was a business
for Carlo Grimes, Clark County resident, described as "Milling corn
grain & others." While the manufacturers census normally reported
businesses in the county where they were located, several lines of
evidence point to this mill of Carlo's being Grimes Mill in Fayette.
No mills are known to have been on the Clark side of Boone Creek
at that time. Carlo had only two deeds purchasing property and only
one deed selling property in Clark County, none of which mentions
a mill.[14] The record is important, since it provides useful details
about the mill's operation just before the war.

According to the census entry, this water gristmill produced
wheat flour and corn meal. The capital investment in the mill was
reported as $3,000. Annual production was 1,200 barrels of flour
and meal from 6,000 bushels of "corn grains and others." One
person was employed to operate the mill. The costs of production

were $2,500 for grain and $12 per month for labor. Sales were $3,000, thus profits were slim.[15] It is unlikely that either Carlo or his brother Charles W. operated the mill day to day, so the "one male" listed as employee would have been their miller.

Carlo Grimes was a solid citizen and businessman. He might have been considered well off financially but not wealthy. Of the twenty nearest farmers in his district in 1850, Carlo was better off than ten, making him about average.[16] He owned nearly 300 acres of land in Clark County. In 1860, his real estate holdings were valued at $6,000 and his personal estate at $6,600. Carlo was obviously well known due to the gristmill. During this period, there was a Grimes Precinct in Clark County.

Charles W. Grimes

Charles William Grimes was born in 1817 on his father's Grimes Mill plantation. He married Mary Ann Embry of Madison County, the thirteenth child of Joel Embry, who had come to Kentucky from North Carolina before the end of the eighteenth century. Several of the Embrys married into the Grimes family. Charles W. and Mary Ann raised fourteen children. In 1850, they were living with his mother in the Grimes House above the mill. After his mother's death, Charles W. and his family lived on in the home. In 1860, Charles W., age forty-three, and Mary Ann, age thirty-nine, had twelve children in their household, ranging in ages from two to nineteen.[17]

Charles W.'s two eldest sons served in John Hunt Morgan's cavalry. Erasmus and Joel Grimes were privates in Colonel Roy Cluke's 8th Kentucky Cavalry. They joined a company commanded by their neighbor, Captain Thomas McCann.[18] The boys enlisted shortly after the nearby battle of Richmond, which saw General Kirby Smith's forces rout the Federal troops in what turned out to be one of the greatest tactical Confederate victories of the war.[19]

According to tradition, the brothers' company passed by Grimes Mill during Cluke's famous Kentucky raid the following year.

Cluke led his cavalry regiment deep into Union-held territory in central Kentucky. With only minor skirmishes along the way, they crossed the Kentucky River in February 1863, at which point many of the men were allowed time to visit their families. Erasmus and Joel were among the fortunate.

> Anxious to see their father, they suggested to Colonel Cluke that they go ahead to the mill and arrange for a meal to be prepared for the regiment and with this permission they eagerly sought the old home, arriving late at night to the surprise and joy of the family. The next day when the regiment arrived great baskets of food were ready waiting for the hungry cavalry men. Many picnics have been held at this beautiful place since then, but never one like that. It was even said that the regiment had the choice of old Grimes' whiskey or water from the famous spring which issues from the cliffs and which has never failed in a hundred years.[20]

Although it sounds wildly improbable that a commander would furlough men on such a perilous mission, Cluke apparently did just that. According to historian Bennett H. Young, at that time one of the soldiers along on the raid, when the regiment reached the Bluegrass, many of the men were allowed to go on leave.

> Cluke's men who lived in the immediate vicinity of Lexington, Mount Sterling, Winchester and Richmond were granted temporary furloughs in order to visit their friends, renew their wardrobes, and if desirable, replace their mounts, and enjoy the association with their loved ones whom they had left four and a half months before. Only the complete mystification and demoralization of his foes could justify so astute a leader as Cluke in risking such a proceeding.[21]

While not providing proof, these details support the plausibility of Cluke's men sojourning at Grimes Mill.

In addition to his inherited property, Charles W. acquired other land near his farm and mill.[22] Then during the Civil War, Carlo and Charles W. Grimes executed an exchange of properties. They went to Winchester on February 16, 1863, where Charles W. sold Carlo the two tracts that he owned in Clark for one dollar.[23] The next day, they went to Lexington, where, also for one dollar, Carlo sold Charles W. all of his interests in the Fayette property that the two brothers held in common—with the exception of the gristmill. The deed excluded

so much of said tract as is occupied by the Mill on Boon Creek and about three acres attached to said Mill and necessary to its occupancy. The said three acres is bounded as follows, commencing at the southwest side of the race at the Mill dam, running thence with the stone quarry to the Mill road till it strikes the stone fence, thence down the said stone fence to the creek, thence with the creek to the Beginning.[24]

This conveyance gave Charles W. sole title to the Grimes House in Fayette County but left the brothers co-owners of the mill.

The timing of these transactions appears to be related to one of Charles W.'s business ventures. On the same day that he obtained title to Carlo's Fayette land, Charles W. mortgaged his property to secure a loan of $4,000 from James Hanna. Charles W. used the inherited land deeded to him by Carlo plus other land he had purchased—about 440 acres in all—as collateral for the loan.[25] He probably used the money to refurbish the mill and construct a distillery.

Grimes Distillery

There is evidence of a small distillery at Grimes Mill pre-dating the Civil War, and there is one reference to the distillery during the war. When Cluke's raiders stopped at the mill, "the regiment had the choice of *old Grimes' whiskey* or water from the famous spring," indicating that a distillery was operating there in 1863.[26] Charles W. got into the whiskey business on a larger scale after the war.

The Civil War would have brought hard times for Grimes Mill if it was still relying on the New Orleans market that had helped make Charles Grimes wealthy. From Union-controlled Kentucky, few goods made their way to the southern states. On the other hand, northern markets were booming. A more serious obstacle was the fact that, by this time, most urban centers had roller mills that could mass produce flour cheaper, faster, and in far greater quantity than water gristmills, which, generally speaking, were on their way to obsolescence. Charles W. may have planned a distillery as a logical complement to his mill. A country mill without ready customers might find new life by using its flour and meal as feedstocks for the production of alcohol. In fact, a distillery was likely to be considerably more profitable than a gristmill. Having a mill already built and directing its output to a distillery would be a further economic advantage to the enterprise.

Grimes' distillery was situated on Boone Creek, about a third of a mile downstream from the gristmill.[27] Though the distance may have been an inconvenience, the location—near an everflowing spring—was essential to operation of the distillery. After the sour mash was heated to boiling, a steady stream of cold, running water had to be passed over the "worm" to condense the alcohol vapor.[28] Next to the distillery, Charles W. built a bonded warehouse, which was required by the Internal Revenue law that went into effect in 1866. It was a place where whiskey could be stored for aging, under the watchful eye of the government, prior to payment of the whiskey tax.

Charles W. may have erected a brand new distillery or renovated and enlarged an old one. The "new" distillery may have been put into operation as early as 1863 and was certainly in production before 1870. Grimes was one of three distillers located in a three-mile stretch of Boone Creek, the others being Poindexter & Pettit and Granville Smitha.[29]

The 1870 manufacturers census for Fayette County listed Charles W. Grimes as listed as the proprietor of a distillery. The record provides some details of Grimes' bourbon-making activities. On the line for Product, the entry was "Copper Distillery," probably referring to the fact that the distillery had a copper still. The business reported an investment of $8,000—twice as much as the gristmill—and employed 5 hands for 5 months. It had a boiler rated at 12 horsepower, indicating that the still was heated with steam. The boiler was fired with coal and wood. The following expenses were itemized for the previous year:

5,000 bushels of corn	$2,000
700 bushels of rye	525
150 bushels of barley	190
40 cords of wood	120
2,800 bushels of coal	556
distillery wages	620
revenue taxes	8,400
total	$12,411

While wood was plentiful on Charles W.'s and Carlo's land, coal had to be hauled up from the Kentucky River.[30] Corn meal, rye flour, and barley flour came from Grimes Mill. The distillery produced 14,000 gallons of whiskey valued at $21,000, nearly six times the value of Grimes Mill's production. After expenses for grain, fuel, labor, and taxes, the distillery turned a profit on paper of about $8,500.[31]

The gristmill was listed in the same manufacturers census, under the name "Grimes & Bro." The mill may have seen some refurbishment too, since the reported capital investment was $4,000, up from $3,000 in the previous census. Its production would have been an important link in the chain after the distillery went into operation.

From other data in the census entry we learn that a 15-foot water wheel turned 2 pairs of millstones with the capacity to grind 200 bushels per day. The water-powered wheel was rated at 20 horsepower. Only 1 employee was required to operate the mill, which ran for 9 months that year. During that period, the mill output—5,625 bushels of corn meal, 790 bushels of rye flour and 170 bushels of barley flour—had a market value of $3,643. However, the census entry stated that the entire production was used for "personal venture," meaning that all the meal and flour were directed to the distillery.[32]   Charles W. and Carlo would have produced much of the grain on their own plantations.

In the 1870 population census, Charles W. Grimes gave his occupation as "farmer and distiller." At the next house, the census taker recorded James W. Lindsay, age forty-eight, occupation "miller," undoubtedly the miller at Grimes Mill. Lindsay's family included wife Mary, age forty, and nine children. This was James William Lindsay who married Mary "Polly" Grimes, the granddaughter of Charles and Jane Grimes. Lindsay was listed in the population census with no real estate or personal property.[33] The manufacturers census listed the mill with a single employee, who was paid $135 for the year. In addition to being Grimes' miller, Lindsay may have been involved in other enterprises with the family. John and James Gess sued Edwin Grimes and William Lindsay for payment for "services performed," an indication that Grimes and Lindsay were business partners.[34]

While the business arrangement between the Grimes brothers at that time is not known, it is clear that they were in the mill and distillery together. They were still co-owners of the mill, and although the distillery was reported in Charles W.'s name, Carlo and others were also involved. Carlo and Henry Gibson gave Charles W. power of attorney

> to sign our names on any bonds as necessary to be executed by said Charles W. Grimes, as a distiller, and all necessary ware house bonds to be executed by said Charles W. Grimes before the proper Revenue Officer.[35]

Another document refers to Charles W. owning one-half interest in the distillery and two-thirds interest in the warehouse.[36]

Financial Misfortunes

Charles W. seemed headed for success in 1870. The mill had run at near capacity, and the distillery had shown a promising, if not surprising, start. His real estate that year was valued at $22,000 and his personal property at $15,775.[37] His star was rising.

Less than two years later, Charles W. faced the first in a series of financial reversals, when he placed all of his real and personal estate in a trust established to pay off his creditors. The remainder, if any, was to be deeded to his wife Mary Ann. This action was the equivalent of taking bankruptcy. The property placed in trust included his real estate in Fayette County, his interest in the distillery, warehouse, and mill, and "some livestock, &c."[38] He appointed William E. Wilkerson as his trustee to dispose of these assets.

The underlying cause of Charles W.'s business problems is not clear. His family had been on the losing side in the war, but the conflict was long over, and besides, Southern sympathy had by then become the dominant feeling in Kentucky.[39] One of the worst business depressions in U.S. history occurred in 1873; however, Charles W.'s problems appear to have begun before then. He may have been overextended by the loans he obtained to build the distillery, upgrade the mill, or invest in other businesses.

Part of his problems stemmed from the whiskey tax laws that went into effect in 1866. In September of that year, the *Lexington Observer and Reporter* noted that there was a "flutter among the distillers," as

> the provisions of the new Internal Revenue law will
> go into effect to-day. In consequences of this a
> large number of whisky distilleries will be closed,
> their owners finding it impossible to continue
> business under the new regime.[40]

Charles W. picked an unfortunate time to get into the whiskey business. In 1868, the distillers of central Kentucky met at the Phoenix Hotel in Lexington to decry the new law that, as they saw it, was

> passed for the special interest of the whisky rings of
> New York, [and] operates with great severity upon
> the distillers of the West.[41]

They claimed the "Whisky Ring" had accumulated a large inventory of illegal, untaxed spirits, and that honest distillers who paid the tax could not compete with them.

The Internal Revenue law of 1865 imposed a $2 per gallon excise tax on whiskey, to be paid at the warehouse before it was shipped. This triggered an explosive increase in the amount of "bootleg" whiskey on the market. In 1868, the tax was reduced to fifty cents per gallon, which was still a significant bite. The price of whiskey in Lexington that year was $3 to $3.50 per gallon.[42] Kentucky distillers claimed that the tax put them at a disadvantage, since the Whiskey Ring, by conspiring with certain revenue collectors, was avoiding the tax and undercutting the price of legal whisky. Overall, the issue subsided when the government broke up the Ring in 1875. The turmoil slowed Kentucky producers very little. Between 1871 and 1880, whiskey production nearly tripled in the state, and by 1882 it doubled again.[43] But while Kentucky bourbon production recovered, many small distillers, including Grimes, went under.

Charles W.'s most obvious problem went back to 1870. For some unexplained reason, he was charged with failure to pay all of the taxes on the whiskey he produced that year, which landed him in trouble with the federal government.[44] The following declaration was made by the Internal Revenue Collector in Lexington:

> Whereas John Prall, assessor of Internal Revenue for the 7th district of Kentucky, did in the year 1870, towit February 1870, assess Charles W. Grimes of Fayette County, Kentucky, who was a resident within said 7th district for *barrel and capacity &c tax due the United States*, and whereas said assessment was duly listed and left with and receipted for by A. H. Bowman, Collector Internal Revenue for the 7th district of Kentucky, and whereas said *Charles W. Grimes failing and refusing to pay said taxes* due the United States as required by law.... [45] (emphasis added)

As a result, the revenue collector Bowman "did distrain and seize upon" one-half acre belonging to Charles W., including all the "appurtenances, fixtures, warehouse &c" and ordered it sold at public auction. Notices were placed in Athens at the post office, in Lexington at the post office and on the courthouse door—and in the Lexington newspaper, the *Kentucky Statesman*:

Public Sale

I will sell to the highest and best bidder on the premises, on Saturday, June 1st, 1872, the Distillery, Distillery Apparatus and Distillery Premises of C. W. Grimes on Boone Creek near Athens, Ky. Said property is sold under Section 42 Act, July 18th, 1866, for nonpayment of taxes and penalties due me as Collector, 7th District, Ky. A. H. Bowman, Collector. By R. P. Stoll, Deputy Collector.[46]

The best bid the Collector received was $551, the "minimum price." The minimum price set by the government may have been the amount of tax Grimes owed, since the deed stated that the property was "sold for taxes." $551 was far too low for a working distillery valued in the manufacturers census two years before at $8,000. The buyer was H. C. Clay, Carlo's son-in-law. Perhaps, no one else showed up to bid. Whatever the reason, it was a lucky break for the family.[47]

H. C. Clay later would achieve some distinction in the whiskey industry of Kentucky. His experience with the Grimes distillery, however, would prove to be disappointing. Although he would continue his involvement in the business, Clay formally assigned his interest back to Charles W., who then made a move to protect the property from his other creditors by deeding the distillery to Mary Ann Grimes. In another instrument the same day, Mary Ann signed an agreement allowing the premises to "be used by E. R. Grimes for the purpose of Distilling Spirits."[48] Edwin R. Grimes was the twenty-six-year-old son of Charles W. and Mary Ann. This latter document, termed a "Consent," was in essence a lease and may have had the effect of further shielding the distillery from Charles W.'s creditors.

This was far from the end of financial problems for Charles W. Grimes. As previously stated, he had committed all of his assets to a trust in the name of William E. Wilkerson. The expressed purpose of the trust was to (1) pay the expenses of the trustee, (2) pay all of Charles W.'s debts, "equally and rateably," and (3) hold the remainder for the "sole and separate use" of Mary Ann Grimes. An itemized inventory of his assets included

> household and kitchen furnitures, Rockaway [carriage] & harness, cows, hogs, wagon & gears, some farming implements, about three Hundred acres of land situate in Fayette County, [and] an undivided half interest in the mill and distillery situate near said land.[49]

The deed of trust was a common device used to execute a bankruptcy. The agreement stated that "the debts [of Charles W.] are far more than can be paid by the personal property" and that it was uncertain how much real estate would have to be sold to pay off the debts. His trustee commissioned a "report of claims" against Charles W. The list of debts amounted to a total of nearly $6,500 owed to twenty-seven creditors. One-third of the amount was owed to relatives, including three of his own sons. In order to execute the trust, Wilkerson filed it with the Fayette circuit court, which styled the case *William E. Wilkerson, trustee of C. W. Grimes vs. C. W. Grimes, Mary A. Grimes his wife, Henry Gibson, Green B. Conody, Carlo Grimes, John Hart, Tarlton Embry, and Henry Clay creditors of C. W. Grimes.* The first transaction under this trust was the sale of Charles W.'s personal estate to his wife Mary Ann for a total of $160. The highest valued items in this sale were "1 four horse wagon" at $50 and "1 Rockaway & Harness" at $10.[50]

Two properties were ordered to be sold at public auction to pay off his creditors. At the first sale, a portion of his farm, just north of the mill, was "knocked down" to William Christian. The second sale involved Charles W.'s one-half interest in the mill property, for which H. C. Clay was the high bidder at $801.[51] Charles W. had now lost his mill, distillery, and most of his land. The only property he still held was the Grimes House and surrounding 75-acre farm. He would not hold on to it for long.

In 1874, Mary Ann Grimes stated in a deposition for *Wilkerson vs. Grimes et al.* that she was "53 years and six months old on the day of the sale [and] I consider my health good." On the same day, Levi Spurr stated, "I have known Charles Grimes all my life and consider his health good [but] judging from appearances the health of C. W. Grimes is not so good as it was a short time ago."[52]

Mary Ann would not outlive her husband, however. She died at home on January 4, 1875. A sentimental obituary in the *Lexington Press*, written in the style of the times, recognized her devotion to church and family.

> For over thirty years Sister Grimes had been a faithful member of the Christian Church, and in every relation of life had so discharged her duty as to win the love and admiration of all who knew her. She was the mother of fourteen children, eleven of whom survive her—seven sons and four daughters. She has left also a devoted husband, a member of the church, who deeply feels his irreparable loss.[53]

She and her husband had been members of the Athens Christian Church since its organization in 1850.[54]

The Grimes House was shown on an 1877 map of Fayette County, labeled "C. W. Grimes."[55] Grimes was still reeling financially, when his stone house and farm were sold in 1878. This sale, like that of the mill, was ordered by the court in continuing actions under *Wilkerson vs. Grimes et al.* to pay off Charles W.'s debts. Talton Embry, brother of Mary Ann Grimes, bought the homeplace.[56] A week later, Embry sold the property to Charles W.'s son, Talton Grimes.[57] Talton was the last Grimes to own the house. Charles W. moved to another home somewhere on the Lexington-Richmond Road. From that point on, the house and mill have been bought and sold as separate properties.

Charles W. Grimes survived his wife by eleven years. He died March 12, 1886. A brief obituary appeared in the *Lexington Morning Transcript*:

> Died

> At his home in this county on Friday night, the 12th
> instant, Charles William Grimes, aged sixty-nine
> years.   Funeral at the house, 12 miles from
> Lexington, Ky., on the Richmond Turnpike, at 11
> o'clock Monday, the 15th of March.[58]

Another short notice printed after the funeral stated that his
"remains were interred in the family burying ground."[59]   Charles
W.'s will was a terse, somewhat unusual document:

> In the name of the Lord Amen, I hereby request that
> the Polacy on my life in the Grange Mutial Benefit
> Sociaty of Kentucky shall be paid over to my three
> daughters to wit Annie, Ruth and Jennie, after
> paying to my sons whatever account they may have
> paid out on this polacy with intrest.
>
> [signed] C. W. Grimes[60]

This "Instrument of writing" was produced in Fayette County court
for probate by Harry Clay (i.e., H. C. Clay), who testified that it was
"wholly in the proper hand writing of said testator." The document
was recorded as the last will and testament of Charles W. Grimes.

After Charles W. Grimes' death, several of his children—
Erasmus, Edwin, Jesse and Orlando—permanently removed to
Alabama. It would be understandable that they wished to leave
behind the bitter family losses and make a new beginning
elsewhere.

One of Charles W.'s sons, William Wallace Grimes, stayed in
Kentucky.   The 1880 manufacturers census listed a distillery
business in Fayette County under the name "W. W. Grimes."[61]
William Wallace may have taken over the distillery after his brother
Edwin went off to Tuscaloosa.   Though not mentioned in the
census, corn meal and flour for the distillery probably came from
Grimes Mill.

The distillery reported a capital investment of $6,000 and three
hired hands. The output of 12,483 gallons of whiskey for 1880 was
only slightly less than the 14,000 gallons reported in 1870. Profits

were slim, however. The cost of production was $4,500 against sales of $6,000.[62]

It is not certain how long the distillery continued to operate, but it was gone before the end of the century when N. W. Embry resided at Grimes House:

> When I lived there in 1898, the distillery had burned, its ruins could be seen between the Grimes' home and Boone's Creek. I recall finding branding irons, used for branding the barrels, in its vicinity.[63]

Only the stone foundation of the distillery survives. The warehouse, as indicated by survey, was located a short distance northwest of the distillery.[64]

Carlo Carries On

Carlo Grimes lived on his farm east of Boone Creek in Clark County from 1838 until 1880. His house on the south side of Grimes Mill Road is no longer standing. The Paris *Western Citizen* reported that Carlo's eldest daughter, Jennie, was married at the house in 1865. She wed the up and coming young H. C. Clay of Bourbon County.[65]

H. C. Clay was a descendant of Henry Clay (1672-1760). This distinguished ancestor of Henrico County, Virginia, was the progenitor of the prominent Clay family of Kentucky. He was the common ancestor of three branches that achieved distinction in the early Commonwealth and included the Honorable Henry Clay of Fayette County, Green Clay of Madison County, and Henry Clay M.D. of Bourbon County. Dr. Henry Clay is recognized as one of the pioneers of Bourbon County. He came to the county in 1787 and reportedly built a stockaded station in the Clintonville District. The following year he built a stone house, which is still standing. H. C. Clay was the great-great-grandson of Dr. Henry Clay.[66]

During the Civil War, H. C. Clay enlisted in the Southern cause and served as a cavalry officer in the First Kentucky Mounted Rifles. Soon after the war ended, he married Carlo Grimes' daughter Jennie.[67]

The setbacks of Charles W. Grimes, in addition to being a concern to the family, must have created a hardship for his brother Carlo. There is no indication, however, that Carlo faced similar financial problems at that time. Fortunately, when Charles W.'s interest in Grimes Mill was sold at public auction, Carlo's son-in-law H. C. Clay was the purchaser. At that time, Carlo and Clay became co-owners, each holding one-half interest in Grimes Mill. They would hang on to the gristmill for twelve more years.

The notion that flowing streams provided a free power supply for mills is quite misleading. It took a lot of money to keep a mill running; i.e., to use the "free" power. Mills required substantial investment to build and significant upkeep to remain in operation. Equipment broke down or wore out, and the damage from flood and fire had to be repaired. This may have been the reason Carlo needed to borrow $3,000 in 1874. He mortgaged his Clark County farm to secure the loan from A. C. Ward, payable at 10 percent interest.[68]

By 1880, Carlo was seventy years old and ready to retire from farming. He and his wife Louisa sold their Clark County farm on Boone Creek, paid off the loan from Ward, and moved to Lexington.[69]

Two years later, Carlo and H. C. Clay may have needed another infusion of cash for the mill, when they borrowed $1,200 from J. W. Appleton. They mortgaged Grimes Mill to secure the loan, payable at 6 percent interest. The note was signed by Carlo Grimes, H. C. Clay, and his wife Jennie Clay, all listed as residents of Lexington. They agreed to keep the mill and all its machinery insured for at least $1,000 with "a good and solvent Company."[70] The note was paid off when it was due, but it took another loan to do so. Carlo and H. C. Clay mortgaged the mill again in order to borrow $1,200, this time at 8 percent interest, from Robert Stone, a director of the Fayette National Bank.[71]

Carlo Grimes died in Lexington in 1883. He did not leave a will. His wife was listed in the 1890 city directory as "Louisa Grimes, widow of Carlo, residence 81 East High Street." Her son Orrin was listed at the same address. Two other sons, Charles P. and John W. Grimes, were living at 416 East High.[72]

The Last Grimes in Grimes Mill

By 1885, Carlo Grimes was dead, H. C. Clay was having financial problems, and the mill was not in the best condition. By then, Grimes Mill was out of the merchant business and distillery business and had become a custom mill for the surrounding area. An insurance policy was issued that year to "H. C. Clay and the heirs of Carlo Grimes." The were insured for

> $600 upon their three story, stone, shingle roofed Building, *operated as a Flour and Grist Mill for neighbourhood custom work only*, conducted by Water Power only, situate on Boones Creek about 12 miles from Lexington in Fayette County, Ky. [and] $400 upon Mill Machinery, Gearing, Belting, Hangers & Pulleys contained in the above observed Mill Building.[73] (emphasis added)

H. C. Clay was a prominent figure in the whiskey industry in Bourbon County and Fayette County. He operated distilleries in Shawhan and Paris as H. C. Clay & Co. He was a principal of Stoll, Clay & Co. in Lexington, which purchased one of Fayette County's largest distilleries. The proprietors were listed as H. C. Clay, R. P. Stoll, and James S. Stoll. His partnership with the Stolls ended acrimoniously, with Clay having to borrow sizeable sums to keep his businesses going.[74]

Clay gave a note to one C. W. Foushee, putting up his share of the gristmill as collateral. When he could not make his payment on the note, Mr. Foushee sued in Fayette circuit court. The court ruled for Foushee and ordered the mill to be sold at public auction to pay the judgment.[75]

At the auction, Robert Stone purchased the "stone flour Mill known as the Grimes Mill property." The same day Stone bought the mill, he conveyed it back to the Grimes family. The deed put ownership of the mill in the name of Mary M. Grimes, who was the wife of Charles P. Grimes.[76] The new owners were Carlo's son and daughter-in-law.

Charles P. Grimes gave Robert Stone a promissory note for the mill. Stone, the banker, should have known better. Unfortunately, Grimes could not meet the loan obligations, and Stone had to sue to collect.[77] With Stone wanting his money and not an aging gristmill, the court ordered the property sold at public auction to pay the debt. A court-ordered appraisal valued the mill and land at only $1,200. To appraise that low, the mill once again must have been in need of substantial repairs. Surprisingly, at the sale Robert Stone was the purchaser, probably due to the fact that the other bids, if any, were so low that he felt he could do better selling the mill on his own.[78]

Stone received a deed from the commissioner of the court on June 8, 1887. On this date, after three generations of the Grimes family operation over a period of eighty years, mill ownership went out of the Grimes family name forever.

Chapter 6

Late Years
1887-1928

A thens entered this period as a diverse and viable community with a population of 350. Its businesses included a dressmaker, undertaker, painter, three hotels, grocer, carpenter, druggist, distiller, livery, harnessmaker, cooper, wagonmaker, blacksmith, and general store. It was also residence to a constable, two justices of the peace, a marshal, and a physician.[1] By this time, many of the Boone Creek industrial sites were returning to wilderness and old families were moving off the land. The Grimes name was about to disappear from the area.

Grimes Mill was not a prospering business at any time during this period. No one representing the mill attended the Kentucky convention of flouring millers held in Lexington in 1888. The mill was not listed in the Kentucky State Gazetteer and Business Directory of 1887 or 1896. No entry appears in the Rural Directory of Fayette County for 1912 or 1926.[2] A search of contemporary newspapers turned up no advertisement of its products.

The mill had a long series of owners succeeding the Grimes family. While the business continued to find buyers, none seemed to be able to make a go of it. One unknown owner made an attempt to increase efficiency and improve winter operation by installing a steel water wheel, but it would be for naught.[3] By the end of the period, Grimes Mill would be the only water-powered gristmill still operating in the county. Unfortunately, long before, it had become an anachronism in the technologically-advanced, Lexington-dominated economy of Fayette County. It was too small, too remote, and too costly to operate and maintain. While stone-ground flour and meal production remained marginally profitable in some rural areas, the "Old Mill" was beginning to fade from the American scene.

Robert Stone

Robert Stone became the sole proprietor of Grimes Mill in 1887. Not wishing to own or run a gristmill, he disposed of the property as soon as he could. It took him nearly two years to do so. Stone sold the mill to Martha McCuddy for $900.[4] Thus began a series of transactions that resulted in the mill changing hands eleven times over the next forty years. It also started a trend of placing the deed in the wife's name. Four of the next eight owners of the mill were women. The purpose, if any, is uncertain, but may have been intended to protect the property from the husband's creditors.

Martha McCuddy

The new owner of Grimes Mill, Martha McCuddy, was identified in the deed as the wife of O. C. McCuddy. An map of Fayette County property owners from that time shows Grimes Mill (labeled as "Mill"). Immediately across the road, a house is shown owned by "T. C. McCuddy" that may have been the residence of Martha and her husband. "T. E. Grimes," owner of the Grimes House at that time, was Talton Embry Grimes.[5]

Mrs. McCuddy was a Grimes descendant. She was the daughter of James William Lindsay and Mary Grimes. Martha's grandfather, Charles Grimes, built the mill. James William Lindsay had been the miller for Charles W. Grimes. McCuddy kept the mill for twenty-three years, longer than any other owner in the late years. By 1912, Martha McCuddy was sixty-two years old, widowed, and had moved to Lexington. That year she sold the establishment to E. B. Wrenn and F. A. Bullock. The sale price of $605 was still coming down.[6] Martha would live thirteen more years, long enough to see her brother become owner of the mill.

Wrenn and Bullock

While Wrenn and Bullock were twice owners of Grimes Mill, nothing about them would indicate any background in flour production or milling. Elias B. Wrenn and his wife Margaret lived on West High Street between 1906 and 1915. He was the partner of Bruce King in Wrenn & King Company, a bookstore at the corner of Main and Mill streets. Frank A. and Grace Bullock were also Lexington residents. Their home was on East Main Street. Frank Bullock was a principal in Skyo Manufacturing Company, a paint manufacturing and wholesaling business, and a long-time judge of the county court.[7] Wrenn and Bullock were in and out of their mill venture in short order.

Nannie Gaitskill

In 1913, only twelve months after they bought it, Wrenn and Bullock sold the mill to Nannie Gaitskill for $2,400 in promissory notes and a house on West 5th Street. The following year, apparently unable to pay off the notes on the mill, Charles W. and Nancy "Nannie" Gaitskill deeded the property back to Wrenn and Bullock for the sum of $2,065. The Gaitskills lived on North Broadway in Lexington from 1902 through 1915. None of the city directories during that period specified an occupation.[8]

Allie Webb

In 1915, eleven months after getting the mill back from the Gaitskills, Wrenn and Bullock sold to Allie Webb for one dollar plus a "certain property" in Lexington that was not identified. All previous transactions involving Grimes Mill had used essentially the same property description found in Carlo Grimes' 1863 deed to Charles W. Grimes.[9] This deed, however, described it somewhat differently. The "stone Flour Mill" known as the "Grimes Mill Property" began at

> a sycamore tree at the North west side of the creek and corner to Eldridge; running thence with the stone fence in a northwesterly direction to the corner of said fence and the stone fence running to the wall of the Mill; thence in northwesterly direction and in a slightly irregular line to the Mill Pond; thence with said pond and the creek and following the meanderings of said creek to the point of the beginning.[10]

The tract was said to contain eight acres, more or less. This deed is also the first to specifically mention the milldam. Wrenn and Bullock transferred "all their right, title and interest in and to the dam across Boones Creek from which the waters are conveyed through the race to the mill."[11] This is an indication that the mill was still in operation at the time of the sale.

Like several other owners before her, Allie Webb was a Lexington resident and did not hold on to the mill for long. At the time she and her husband owned the mill, they lived on Warren Court. Richard Webb Jr. owned a contractor business with his father under the name of R. S. Webb and Company. Richard Jr. later owned an automobile repair business, the Mammoth Garage on East Main Street.[12]

Charles Lindsay

The Webbs sold Grimes Mill to Charles C. Lindsay in 1916, for which they received $2,590 in promissory notes. The Webbs retained a lien on the property and "all the machinery of whatsoever kind now contained in said mill building." Lindsay was required to insure the mill and machinery for not less than $2,000. Since the deed was made "subject to existing leases," the Webbs may have been leasing the mill to someone else to operate at the time Lindsay bought the mill.[13]

Charles Lindsay was the younger brother of Martha McCuddy and the last known Grimes descendant to own the mill. Charles was fifty-nine years old when he purchased the business, an advanced age to begin milling if he was not acquainted with the profession. Although his occupation was given as farmer, the city directory listed Charles and his wife Fannie as residents of Lexington between 1919 and 1927. Their home was on Walton Avenue, so it is unlikely he was personally running the mill at that time.[14]

George Kirby

Charles Lindsay kept the mill for about four and a half years before selling two-thirds interest to George Kirby in 1921. Kirby agreed to pay a note for $2,400 owed by Lindsay. Lindsay had made little progress paying off this note, reducing the principal by only $190 in five years. The following year, Lindsay conveyed his remaining one-third interest to Kirby for $500.[15]

Given that every owner after the McCuddys lived in Lexington, it seems unlikely that any of them served as a resident miller. That pattern was broken by the Kirbys, who lived in the county. George and Lillie Kirby lived on Bennett Pike in 1912; he was listed in the rural directory as a fence contractor. They later moved to town. In 1925, he was listed in the city directory as a coal dealer, and two years later as a lumberman.[16] It is not safe to say whether this versatile background qualifies him as a candidate for miller. If he served in that capacity, however, it was only for a short period of time. His tenure as owner lasted less than two years.

Annie Bowen

In 1923, Kirby exchanged properties with Y. C. Bowen and his wife Annie. The Bowens traded two lots in Lexington for Grimes Mill. The mill was entered on the deed in Annie Bowen's name.[17] In this manner, York Bowen became the last proprietor to operate the facility as a gristmill. He kept Grimes Mill going until 1928.

Y. C. "York" Bowen was from Powell County. He was born during the Civil War in the community of Bowen, named for his ancestors and later renamed "Filson" for the railroad station there. York, the son of William and Mary Bowen, had been a brickmaker and jailer in Powell County before moving to Lexington in 1912. York Bowen was listed in the city directory that year with wife Annie, son Charles, and daughter Mary. His occupation was reported as carpenter, his address West 5th Street. The year he bought the mill, York was listed in the city directory as a blacksmith with his residence on Sherman Avenue. He would not be listed in the directory again until after he sold the mill.[18]

York himself had a distant sort of Grimes connection. His daughter, Mary Bowen (listed as Mae in the city directories), married Frank Mischler Jr. Frank, a lathe operator and a life-long resident of Lexington, was the son of Frank and Katherine Mischler. At one time, Frank Jr. and his widowed mother owned one-half interest in the Grimes House, which they purchased from the Eldridge family. It is uncertain whether or not the Mischlers ever lived there.[19]

York would have been sixty-one years old at the time he purchased Grimes Mill and sixty-six by the time he sold it. Since no experience in the flouring trade shows up in his background, it is a little surprising that he would begin a milling career at an age when many people are beginning to think of retirement.

In one of the last accounts of Grimes Mill operation, the *Clay City Times* reported that Bowen, the "old residenter," was back home for a few days of socializing.

Y. C. Bowen, a former officer of Powell county,
and an ever pleasant gentleman, is in the county for
a visit to old friends. His son, Charlie Bowen,
drove up Monday with him, but has returned to
Lexington where he [Charlie] operates a wall paper
and decorative store.

The newspaper article indicates that Bowen was closely involved
with the mill's superintendence, stating that "Mr. Y. C. Bowen
operates the old Grimes' Mills, one of the few remaining water
wheel buhr mills." Mr. John E. Burgher wrote the article, which
went on to give valuable information on Grimes Mill's final years of
production:

[Bowen] has both wheat and corn stones, and
makes whole wheat flour. He supplies hospitals
and sick people in general with flour, where doctors
find the white flour is injurious to them. The editor
is particularly fond of the kind of flour he makes,
but rarely ever gets any of this kind, since the old
Forge mill here in Clay City ceased to operate in the
fall of 1888.

We are intending to go down to visit for a day our
good friend York Bowen at Grimes' Mill where we
can see that 28-foot over shot water wheel revolve
as did the old Forge wheel when we were a lad, in
sight of where The Clay City Times is now printed.
We anticipate seeing old-time milling by an old-
time friend will bring to us fondest memories of the
happy past.

The mill house where Mr. Bowen owns is a three-
story rock structure and was built in 1803, is
therefore 124 years old.[20]

The article reports that the Bowen had two pairs of millstones, one
pair for grinding wheat and one pair for corn. The erroneous
construction date is the one given in nearly every story about
Grimes Mill. Most of the other facts check out, except the diameter
of the water wheel. The wheel pit cannot accommodate a water

wheel much larger than the 16 ½-foot steel wheel that is still in place inside the mill.

Although the notion of bleached white flour being unhealthy sounds like a modern idea, it was actually part of the "pure food movement" of the early 1900s.[21] More importantly, the story suggests that Bowen's mill was producing flour for a very small specialty market. The country miller's dilemma is illustrated by the editor's personal experience—he enjoys the stone-ground flour for its taste as well as the nostalgia, but rarely eats it. Rather than travel to a rural mill, most people bought flour and meal in town, where the cheaper, mass-produced products of roller mills were sold.

Less than a year after the *Clay City Times* article, the old gristmill would close. In the spring of 1928, the Bowens sold Grimes Mill to the Iroquois Realty Company. The head gates were closed one last time. As water was diverted from the millrace, the overshot wheel slowed and stopped. The millstones ground to a halt. After 120 years of operation, the mill fell silent. The building, however, began a new life and carries on today as the home of the Iroquois Hunt Club.

Chapter 7

Iroquois Hunt Club

The first Iroquois Hunt was organized in 1880 by General Roger D. Williams.[1] The name derives, not from the from the famed Native-American confederacy, but from the first American-bred horse to win the English Derby—Pierre Lorillard's Iroquois.[2] Williams based his hunts on English tradition but varied them to suit the Kentucky setting. The hunts were conducted at various Bluegrass farms in Fayette, Clark, and Madison counties. While foxhunting was the main attraction, rabbit hunts and coon hunts were also popular. According to Fauntleroy Pursley, the Hunt "flourished in the nineties [but] disbanded in 1914 when 'wars and rumors of wars' made it impracticable to carry on."[3]

The club became active again after World War I and was formally reorganized at the Ashland Club (now Idle Hour Country Club) on November 6, 1926, and the following day twenty-three members "met in the oak-studded meadows of Ashland to take part in a paper chase." The first hunt was held a few weeks later on Thanksgiving Day. L. B. Shouse and Kendall McDowell were named joint Masters of Fox Hounds.[4] The masters were responsible for maintaining the pack of hounds and for directing the hunts. The dogs were all Walker foxhounds, descended from a strain developed by John Walker and George Maupin. The excitement and thrill of the chase is vividly portrayed in the following account of a hunt in those early years:

> For two and a half hours hounds gave tongue like nothing human, circled Gentry's cliffs four times. Field of twenty five, all thrusters. Viewed fox with one hound running sight race and others close behind. Fox foiled them and slipped off. Wonder to see hound work picking up scent, then off like magic. Fox lay down behind stone wall once and waited till hounds went by. After two and half hours, fox tired and managed to go to ground in

cliff with almost every hound there and every member of the field.[5]

Soon after reorganization, the club began seeking permanent headquarters for its members. In 1928, the club bought Grimes Mill and eight acres of land from Y. C. and Annie Bowen for $5,000 in promissory notes and "other considerations."[6] Hunt secretary, John Gourlay, reported the purchase in a letter he wrote to club members:

> Upon the practically unanimous vote of all those of the Hunt who accepted the invitation to the dinner meeting held in the Lafayette Hotel Ballroom on the evening of the 7th instant, your officers have proceeded to purchase the Grimes Mill property for the use of the Hunt. In accordance with the plan stated at that meeting, the property was bought at the price of $9,270, and a holding corporation of the non-profit kind... was organized under the name "Iroquois Realty Company" to take and hold the title to the property.[7]

As Gourlay explained, the club's transaction was staked by a loan from John Pursley:

> Five thousand dollars of the purchase price was lent to the corporation by that good friend of the Hunt, Mr. John G. Pursley of Clark County, upon the corporation's notes, secured by lien on the property. The rest of the purchase price was raised upon subscriptions of members of the Hunt, each subscriber becoming entitled to a 'membership certificate' (instead of a share of stock) for each $100 subscribed and paid by him into the corporate treasury.[8]

Gourlay added that another $3,000 needed to be raised to build a kennel, renovate the stable, and "for a few necessary repairs to the stone building in order to make it usable as a clubhouse."

For the first time in years, Grimes Mill was newsworthy. Its purchase by the Hunt Club prompted front-page coverage and a picture in the Sunday *Lexington Herald*. The headline announced "Iroquois Hunt Club Buys Grimes Mill." The article mentioned their plan to use "a *portion* of the mill... as a clubhouse for members" and suggested that milling operations would continue.

> The machinery of the mill will not be disturbed and it is hoped that for many years to come, as the water flows over the wheel, that the famous meal and flour will continue to flow into the bins.[9]

Alas, it was not to be. The plan may have been inconsistent with the club's use of the facility. Perhaps more importantly, it was economically impractical. At some point, most of the mill machinery was removed and the long millrace filled in.[10] The water wheel remains in place, though some of its buckets have rusted away. From the outside, the only visible clue that the building once housed a gristmill is the pair of millstones used to decorate the front entrance.

The milldam across Boone Creek survived for a few years before it was washed away during a flood. Included in the loss was a swimming hole that had served the neighborhood for many generations.[11]

Although the Iroquois Hunt Club has made a number of alterations and additions to the property and to the stone mill itself, it has won praise for preserving the historic building. Rather than attempt a costly restoration project, the club made a diligent effort to conserve the existing structure. The stone walls, three feet thick in places, were left exposed on the interior, as were the massive timbers used in the posts and beams. After standing for nearly two hundred years, the original stonework and wood are still in excellent condition.

Some renovation and repair work has been necessary over the years. Old window sashes were replaced, new flooring was laid on the first and second stories, and more convenient stairs to the basement and second floor were installed. A floor was built over the water wheel pit, and that area now houses the kitchen. The roof was repaired and some of the attic framing on the third level was replaced. A number of improvements were made in 1962, when a 20 by 50 foot room was added on the east side of the mill, with dressing rooms beneath it, and a swimming pool was finished in 1963.[12] The clubhouse is now used as a year-round facility.

The Iroquois Hunt Club saved Grimes Mill. Under their tenure, the mill has become the scene of a long-running ritual enacted along Boone Creek. Each fall the rolling hills and cliffs come alive with sights and sounds of the foxhunt. These picturesque events are always newsworthy and are dutifully reported by local scribes.[13]

The season opens with the Blessing of the Hounds, an old British custom dating back to the days of St. Hubert, the patron saint of huntsmen. The blessing was instituted by the Iroquois Hunt Club in 1931 and has been conducted ever since. The hunts begin in early fall and continue through early spring.

After nearly three-quarters of a century of club ownership, Grimes Mill is now firmly established as the icon of the Iroquois Hunt. In the public perception, the old mill is the home of a prestigious club, rather than a defunct business establishment. This is to be hailed, not mourned. The metamorphosis of the old mill into club headquarters gave it new life, without which it would likely have suffered the fate of hundreds of other Kentucky mills—ruin and destruction. Instead of shedding its old image, the mill has become part of another heritage, the 120-year old Hunt Club. With the club, Grimes Mill enjoys a celebrated existence that was unthinkable as a struggling flour mill. With the approach of hunting season each autumn, it moves to center stage. Many participate in the festivities, and others come to watch. Still others attend to write about it. Jobie Arnold did the honors in 1962:

> You can't beat the color and traditional pageantry seen yesterday at the Iroquois Hunt Club's Blessing of the Hounds. Seventy-five pink and black coated riders accepted the coveted St. Hubert's medallion from the Rev. Wm. R. Moody, in front of the beautiful old stone Iroquois Club house on the Grimes Mill Road. A handsome pack of English-Walker Hounds sat quietly in front of Iroquois Joint Masters W. F. Pursley and Ed Spears as they were blessed for the winter hunting season, and handsomely braided horses nickered and tramped in the background, eager to be off for the chase.[14]

The story went on to name Joker and Finder as two of the top hounds in the pack.

Except for many new names, it was much the same in the fall of 2000, when Bishop Stacy Sauls performed the blessing, Vicky Walker was Hunt Club president, Jack van Nagell was huntmaster, and Jerry Miller was huntsman. Rascal and Fickle were among the top hounds. And Holly Stepp answered the challenge of finding a new way to describe the annual ritual. She played her story, "Steeped in Tradition," from the angle of the hounds:

> Talk about a dog's life. Imagine getting to spend your days on lush a Fayette County farm.... Then fall comes, and it's your time to shine. Thirty of you get to tear across the hills in search of the elusive fox, and you get a blessing to boot. Talk about hound heaven.[15]

And so Grimes Mill has endured in the land of Daniel Boone—located on the creek bearing his name, two and a half miles from his station and four miles from Fort Boonesborough. The old mill is now recognized as a Kentucky landmark and deserving of its own place in the state's rich cultural history.

Iroquois Hunt Club after remodeling, c1931.
(Lafayette Studio Collection, Courtesy University of Kentucky)

Blessing of the hounds. (Lafayette Studio Collection, Courtesy
University of Kentucky)

Epilogue

Each year more of Kentucky's historic landmarks disappear forever, falling victim to the wrecking ball, vandalism, or lack of attention. The "Old Mill" has gone the way of the pioneer forts, the iron furnaces, and the covered bridges. Although the gristmill played a critical role in the early Commonwealth, only a handful survive today. Weisenberger Mill on South Elkhorn Creek in Woodford County is the only commercial, water-powered gristmill still in business. Its turbines produce stone-ground flour and meal the old-fashioned way. Two mills are run on a part-time basis— Mill Springs Mill near Lake Cumberland in Wayne County and the reconstructed McHargue's Mill in Levi Jackson State Park in Laurel County. Two other mills remain more or less intact with their machinery in place—Wolf Pen Mill at Prospect in Jefferson County and Green Brothers Mill at the Falls of Rough in Grayson County.

As it approaches its second century mark, Grimes Mill on Boone Creek not only endures but has the good fortune to be in excellent condition and to have owners committed to its preservation. No one knows how many other mills are still standing around the state. Documentation of this once important industry is sadly lacking and sorely needed.[1] Much more effort is wanted in order to save this vanishing symbol of Americana from progress and neglect.

Appendices

A.
Glossary of Mill-Related Terms

BED STONE—The bottom millstone, the one remains stationary, below the runner stone.

BOLTER—A machine for bolting (sifting) flour to remove the bran and other course matter; sometimes called a bolting chest. Often used silk cloth as a screen. The product is referred to as "bolted flour."

BOLTING—The process of sifting flour into varying grades of fineness.

BUHR—A term used at one time for a segmented millstone (e.g., French buhrs) and later applied to millstones in general.

BURR—See BUHR.

CUSTOM MILL—A gristmill where local farmers brought their grain for grinding. In return for grinding, the miller retained a percentage or "toll" of the product.

GATE—A device to control the flow of water into the millrace (head gate) or the sluice (sluice gate).

GRIST—The term was used interchangeably to describe the grain brought to a mill for grinding as well as the ground products of a mill.

GRISTMILL—A facility for grinding grains, most often corn and wheat, to produce meal or flour.

HEAD—The vertical distance of water fall measured from the end of the sluice to the bottom of the water wheel—or the level of the water, if the water wheel was partly submerged. The head is one of the factors that determines the available horsepower at a mill site.

HEAD GATE—A gate that could be opened and closed to control the flow of water from the millpond to the millrace.

MERCHANT MILL—A gristmill whose products, usually flour by the barrel, were produced for the wholesale market.

MILL—In the eighteenth century, this term was used to describe any machinery used for grinding or any machinery powered by animal, water, or wind. The water-powered machinery included devices for turning, sawing, beating, mixing, crushing, spinning, and so on.

MILLDAM—A dam built across a stream to serve a mill by (1) raising the water level to provide head and (2) storing water to provide a steady flow.

MILLPOND—The backwater formed behind a milldam.

MILLRACE—A man-made channel for carrying water from the millpond to the water wheel, also referred to as the race.

MILLSTONES—Circular stones, containing furrows cut into the flat surface, that worked in pairs to pulverize grain. The top stone (runner stone) rotated, and the bottom stone (called the bed stone or nether stone) was fixed. Grain was introduced via a hole in the center of the runner stone and product emerged around the outer edges.

OVERSHOT WATER WHEEL—A water wheel that is powered by water pouring over the top of the wheel. The weight of water in the buckets turns the wheel. The Fitz Water Wheel Company manufactured a version that they referred to as their "steel overshoot water wheel."

RACE—See MILLRACE.

ROLLER MILL—A modern variety of mill in which the grain is pulverized between two horizontal metal rollers in much the same way that the clothes-wringer worked on an old-fashioned washing machine.

RUNNER STONE—The top millstone, the one that revolves above the bed stone.

SLUICE—A wooden box for carrying water from the end of the millrace to the water wheel, often running above ground level and supported on piers.

SLUICE BOX—See SLUICE.

SLUICE GATE—A gate that could be opened and closed to control the flow of water from the sluice to the water wheel.

TAILRACE—A man-made channel to carry water from the wheel pit back to the stream.

WATER WHEEL—A circular wheel made with regularly-spaced paddles or buckets around the perimeter. The water wheel was placed where flowing or falling water could be used to turn the wheel. The water wheel worked in concert with the power train—a system of axles and gears—to turn the millstones.

WHEEL PIT—A four-sided enclosure used at some mills to protect the water wheel from the elements.

B.
Documents

The conclusions reached in this work are notably different in certain aspects from the prevailing historical tradition regarding the building of Grimes Mill. In order to support the argument, it is necessary to present some of the critical evidence used in reaching this alternative viewpoint. To this end, the most relevant primary sources are transcribed below.

Deed Conveying the Mill Tract to Winn and Grimes
1805

Fayette County Circuit Court Deed Book B

pp. 335-36   This Indenture made and concluded on the fourth day of May in the year of our Lord one thousand eight hundred and five by and Between Eli Cleveland and Mary his wife of the one part and John Winn Jr. and Charles Grimes of the other part, all of Fayette County and Kentucky state, Witnesseth That the said Eli Cleveland and Mary his wife for and in consideration of fifty Pounds cash to them in hand paid have this day Bargained and sold and by these presents do Bargain and sell unto the said John Winn Jr. and Charles Grimes as tenants in common one certain Tract or parcel of land containing sixty acres and thirty poles by survey, be the same more or less, Laying on Boons Creek in the County of Fayette and Bounded as followeth Towit: Beginning at two white oaks and elm and running Thence South thirty five Degrees East thirty two poles to a White Walnut and box Elder on Boons Creek, running thence with the middle and meanders of said Creek North eighty six Degrees East seventy poles, Thence South sixty three Degrees East twenty poles, Thence North seventy eight Degrees East forty six poles, Thence

North thirty two [degrees] East thirty one poles,
Thence North thirty five [Degrees] West eighteen
poles, Thence North forty three Degrees West
eleven poles, Thence South eighty eight Degrees
West fifteen poles, Thence South seventy nine
Degrees West thirty six poles to the top of clift to a
White oak and Iron wood, Thence with the
meanders of the clift North sixty five Degrees
[west] twenty two poles, Thence North twenty two
Degrees West forty four poles, Thence North seven
Degrees East twenty four poles to two Black oaks
and hickory, Thence South forty seven Degrees
West two hundred & three poles to a hickory,
Thence North sixty four and one half Degrees East
to the Beginning, Together with all ways, woods,
water courses, mines, minerals, quarries and all and
any of its appurtenances of every kind thereunto
belonging or in any wise appurtaining, To have and
to hold the said Tract of Land as tenants in common
for the only proper use of them the said John Winn
Jr. & Charles Grimes and their heirs forever and the
said Eli Cleveland and Mary his wife do by these
presents acknowledge and confess themselves fully
satisfied and paid by the said John Winn and
Charles Grimes for the premises hereby Bargained
and sold and hereby conveyed unto the said John
Winn Jr. and Charles Grimes as tenants in common
and doth hereby exonerate and discharge the said
John Winn Junior and Charles Grimes and their
heirs forever and the said Eli Cleveland and Mary
his wife do by these presents bind themselves, their
heirs, &c to warrant and defend the right and title of
the aforesaid tract of land and every part and parcel
thereof with all its appurtenances thereunto
belonging or in any wise appurtaining unto the said
John Winn Junior and Charles Grimes as Tenants in
common and their heirs forever from the claim of
all and every person or persons whatsoever, In

Testimony of which we have hereunto affixed Our hands and seals the day and Year before Written.
Teste:

| Leonard K. Bradley | Eli Cleveland [signed] |
| Hezekiah Harrison | Mary Cleveland [her mark] |

I John Poindexter do hereby Certify that twenty acres three rods and thirty five poles of the land contained in this deed was sold by me to John Winn Junior and Charles Grimes and the title being in Eli Cleveland from whom I Purchased it do authorize him to convey it to said Winn and Grimes and this quantity is to be reducted out the Quantity of land which I formerly purchased of Eli Cleveland being two Hundred acres which said Cleveland made me a Deed for which was consumed by fire in Fayette office. Given under my hand and seal this 4th of May 1805.
Teste:

| Hezekiah Harrison | John Poindexter [signed] |
| Leonard K. Bradley | |

*A plot of this tract (**see map on page 15**) confirms that this land lies in the bend of Boone Creek where the mill was built.*

Winn and Grimes Mill Petitions, Etc.
1805-1810

Fayette County Order Book 1
May 1, 1805
p. 277   Winn & Grimes Mill

On the motion of John Winn and Charles Grimes for leave to build a water grist mill on Boons Creek in the county of Fayette they owning the lands on both sides of said creek where the said mill is proposed to be built; Ordered that a writ of ad quod damnum issue, to be executed according to law on the 28th Instant, and return thereof made to Court according to law.

Fayette County Order Book 1
June 20, 1805
p. 290   Winn & Grimes Mill
                  On the petition of John Winn & Charles Grimes for
                  leave to erect a dam to work a water grist and saw
                  mills on Boons creek in Fayette County, they
                  owning the land on one side of said creek only
                  where the same is to be built; Ordered that a writ of
                  ad quod damnum issue, to be executed agreeable to
                  law on the 13th instant, and report thereof made to
                  Court according to Law.

Fayette County Order Book 1
August 12, 1805
p. 310   Winn & Grimes Mill
                  The Sheriff this day made return of the report of the
                  Jury on the mill of John Winn and Charles Grimes;
                  Ordered that summons be awarded against Adam
                  Winn and William Ford to appear at next Court and
                  show cause why the same may not be established.

Fayette County Order Book 1
October 14, 1805
p. 320   Winn & Grimes Mill
                  The sheriff made report to Court of a writ of ad
                  quod damnum, together with the Jurys report
                  thereon, obtained by John Winn and Charles
                  Grimes, thereupon the same is Ordered to be
                  quashed, they refusing to build their mill on the
                  conditions mentioned therein.

Fayette County Order Book 1
November 11, 1805
p. 331   Winn & Grimes Mill
                  On the petition of John Winn and Charles Grimes,
                  they proving notice of this motion being given to
                  William Ford; Ordered that a Writ of Ad quod
                  damnum issue directed to the Sheriff to impannell a
                  Jury to meet on the 23rd Instant November on their

land on Boons Creek for the purpose of assessing damages and condemning one acre of land the property of William Ford against which land they wish to abut a dam for working a water grist mill, they owning the land on the other side of said creek, and make report thereof to Court.

Fayette County Order Book 1
March 9, 1807
p. 444

Winn & Grimes Mill
On the motion of John Winn and Charles Grimes who are desirous of erecting a dam to work a water Grist mill on Boons creek, they owning the lands on one side only; Ordered that a writ of Ad quod damnum issue, for a Jury to meet on the said premises on the 11th day of April next to enquire and make report agreeable to law.

Fayette County Order Book 1
April 13, 1807
p. 451

Winn & Grimes Mill
A Report of Inquest on John Winn and Charles Grimes writ of Ad quod damnum was returned to Court and Ordered that a summons issue against William Winn to appear at next court and show cause why the same may not be established agreeable to the report of the Jury.

The jury met at John Winn's and Charles Grimes' property on April 4, 1807, but their "Report of Inquest," referred to above, was not accepted and recorded by the court until October 1810 (see below).

Fayette County Order Book 1
May 11, 1807
p. 461

Winn & Grimes Mill
Ordered that the Report of Winn and Grimes Writ of Ad quod damnum be Continued untill next Court.

Fayette County Order Book 2
October 8, 1810
pp. 293-94   Winn & Grimes Mill
Report of a Jury on a Writ of Add Quodd Damnum
on Winn and Grimes Mill having been returned and
William Winn being Summoned to show cause
against its establishment the said Winn appeared
and by his consent the Court confirmed said report
and establishes the Mill accordingly which is
ordered to be recorded and is in the following
words, to wit:
"Fayette County Sct. In pursuance of a Writ of ad
quod damnum directed to the Sherriff of said
County requiring him to Summon & attend with
twelve fit persons on the Land of John Winn and
Charles Grimes on Boons Creek where they desire
erecting a Damm for the purpose of working a
water grist and Saw Mills, as Jurors to enquire and
report as the Law directs. I Charles Carr, Sherriff
of said County have convened on said Land with
the subscribing Jurors on the 4th day of May 1807
as directed and there duly charged them agreeable
to Law. And the said John Winn and Charles
Grimes owning the Land on one side only of said
Creek, the said Jurors have circumscribed and laid
off by metes and bounds one acre of Land on the
opposite side, the property of William Winn,
according to the charge given and the Law
concerning Mill Dams, and other obstruction of
Water courses." (a survey of which is herewith
enclosed) And having due regard to the Interest of
both parties have appraised the same according to
its true value to be worth seven Dollars. They have
also examined the lands above and below the
property of others, and are of opinion that if there
be a Dam erected across the said creek from five
feet ten Inches to six feet high from the bed thereof
it will damage the said William Winn not in any

manner. And we do further report that it will injure no other person, nor the mansion house, office, curtiledge or gardens of any person, nor the orchard of any person will be injured by the overflowing of the water, that no Fish of passage or ordinary navigation will be obstructed. And we are further of opinion that the Health of the neighbours will not be annoyed by the erection of said dam or stagnation of the water. In Witness thereof we have hereunto set our hands & seals this 4th day of April 1807.

William Davenport	James Whaley
John McCall	John Poindexter
William Cotton	Stephen Lay
Robert Marshall	Robert Boggs
Edward Bullock	James Allen
Thomas Clark	Hal Jenkins

Test   Charles Carr S.F.C.

[Survey] Begining at Poindexters Corner at a hickory white oak and ceddar on Boons Creek, thence South 79 W. 36 poles to the topp of the Clift to a white oak and Iron Wood, thence N. 19 East 9 poles to a large Rock in the bed of the Creek, thence down the Creek to the begining, Containing one Acre.

Grimes Mill Road Orders
1808-1810

Fayette County Order Book 1
April 10, 1808
pp. 528-29   New Road

On the application of Charles Grimes, It is ordered that Stephen Lay, William Cotton, Robert Marshall, and Isaac Tinsley be and they are hereby appointed commissioners to view the ground on which a new road is proposed to be opened from Cleaveland road by the stone meeting House to the mill of said

Charles Grimes, also from the same road near to William Cottons to said Grimes mill and report of the conveniences and inconveniences that will result as well to Individuals as the publick if said roads should be opened.

Clark County Order Book 4, 1805-1812
July Court 1808
pp. 257-58   On Motion of Charles Grimes Ordered that Leonard Hill, James Gibson, Henry Heronimous and John Morton or any three of them Being first sworn do view the nearest and best way for a Road from the ford of Boons Creek opposite Charles Grimes Mill to where it will intersect Rogers road leading from German Town to Rogers Mill and make Report of the Conveniences and inconveniences attending the same to the Court.

Fayette County Order Book 2, 1808-1811
July 11, 1808
p. 25   Grimes mill road
The report of the commissioners who were appointed to view Charles Grimes mill road was this day returned and ordered that a summon issue to the sheriff of this County directing him to summon Eli Cleaveland and John Poindexter "proprietors of the land thru which said road is proposed to [be] conducted" to appear here at the next Court and show cause if any they can why said road shall not be opened agreeable to said report.

Fayette County Order Book 2
August 8, 1808
p. 32   Charles Grimes mill road
The report of the viewers of Charles Grimes mill road was returned at last Court and a summon issued to Eli Cleaveland and John Poindexter proprietors of the land through which said road will run was returned,

executed and said Poindexter appearing in Court and objecting to said road being opened.

On the motion of said Charles Grimes ordered that a Writ of Ad Quod damnum issue to the sheriff of this County directing the sheriff to summon a Jury to meet at the place at which said road first strikes the line of said Poindexters land on the 22nd day of August Instant to assess damages and report thereon agreeable to law to next Court. Eli Cleaveland the other proprietor of the land thru which said road will run consents to its being opened.

Clark County Order Book 4
October Court 1808

pp. 277-78   A Report of a road from the ford of Boons Creek opposite Charles Grimes Mill to where it will intersect Rogers road leading from German Town to Rogers Mill returned and established according to said Report.

Ordered that Henry Heronimous be appointed overseer of the road from the ford of Boons Creek opposite Charles Grimes Mill to where it will intersect Rogers Road leading from German Town to Rogers Mill.

Ordered that Leonard Hill and James Gibson allott the hands to Work under Henry Heronimous overseer thereof.

Fayette County Order Book 2
October 10, 1808

p. 47   Grimes mill road
The report of a Jury on a writ of Ad quod Damnum awarded Charles Grimes on his mill road was returned to Court and ordered to be recorded, which is in the following words:
By virtue of a writ of Ad quod Damnum hereto anexed we the subscribers having been this day

summoned and impaneled by John H. Morton Sheriff of Fayette County and charged on oath agreeable to law have viewed and examined the land of John Poindexter through which a road from Charles Grimes Mill is proposed to be conducted, and we are of opinion that said road will pass through said John Poindexters land about 700 yards, and that Poindexter will sustain damage to the amount of Ten dollars by reason of said road passing through his land. In Witness whereof we have hereunto set our hands and seals this 22nd day of August 1808.

Jeremiah Rogers	John Hendly
Robert Marshall	Dennis Bradley
Alexander Crawford	George Stapleton
William Devanport	James Bently
Thadius Dulin	Joseph Bradburn
Thomas Ferguson	Robert Boggs

That said [road] be opened & established at said Grimes expence.

p. 50   Grimes mill road
Ordered that Charles Grimes be appointed overseer of Grimes mill road to open and keep said road in repair. Edmund Bullock and William Davenport are appointed to allot him hands for the purpose aforesaid.

Clark County Order Book 4
July Court 1809
p. 324   On motion of Charles Grimes Ordered that Lewis Grigsby, Gholson Bush, Harvey Quisenberry and Jesse Banten or any three of them being first sworn do view the nearest and best way for a road from Grimes Mill Road where it intersects Rogers Road from thence to intersect Heronimous Road [illegible] to where it goes down the Hill to Heronimous ware house and make Report thereof to

the court of the conveniences and inconveniences attending the same as well to the publicks as the individuals.

Fayette County Order Book 2
April 9, 1810
p. 250   Poindexter v Grimes

On motion of John Poindexter It is ordered that a summons issue to the Sheriff of this county directing him to summon Charles Grimes to appear here at next Court to shew cause, if any he can, why he has not paid to him the said Poindexter the damages which was adjudged him by a Jury on a Writ of Ad Quod damnum granted said Grimes.

Fayette County Order Book 2
November 13, 1810
p. 314   Grimes Mill Road

Ordered that Henry Walker be and is hereby appointed Overseer of Charles Grimes Mill road, in the room of Charles Grimes resigned. Richard Bledsoe and Robert Marshall to allott him hands to keep it in repair as the Law direct.

C.
Grimes Family History

This family history beginning with Nicholas Grimes of Loudoun County, Virginia, is far from complete. It is intended to give a genealogical context for understanding the Grimes family members involved with Grimes Mill. Thus, after Phillip Grimes (second generation), descendants are not given for individuals who have no connection to the mill. The family list below is built upon and extends the work of many previous genealogy studies.[1]

An asterisk before the name indicates that the individual's family appears in the next generation. Grimes Mill owners' names appear in italics. Many of the birth dates are taken from census data and therefore should be considered approximations.

First Generation

Nicholas Grimes
  b. 1690[2]
  d. 1766 in Loudoun County, Virginia
  m. 1714, Sarah Donaldson

  Children of Nicholas and Sarah:[3]
  Sarah Grimes
  William Grimes
  Edward Grimes
  *Phillip Grimes
  Nicholas Grimes[4]
  Jemima Grimes

Second Generation

Phillip Grimes
  b. 1734 in Virginia or Maryland
  d. February 26, 1806 in Fayette County
  m. Mary Dowdall (1728-1796) in Virginia

Children of Phillip and Mary:[5]

Mary Grimes (c1758-1790) m. William Payne

John Grimes m. Mrs. Valinda Cotton Bates

James Grimes (1760-1828) m. (1) Jemima Neal and (2) Sarah Bryan, 1787

Stephen Grimes (b. 1763) m. (1) Margaret England, 1778 and (2) Sarah Garrard, 1789

Avory Grimes (1765-1815) m. Elizabeth Bates

Benjamin Grimes (1767-1836) m. Anna Talbott

Phillip Grimes (b. 1769)

Charles Grimes

Third Generation

Charles Grimes

b. 1771 in Loudoun County, Virginia

d. August 8, 1837 in Fayette County

m. 1791, Jane Winn (1775-1856) in Fayette County

Children of Charles and Jane:[6]

*Mary "Polly" Grimes

*John Grimes

Charles Grimes (1798-1801)

Phillip Grimes (1801-c1801)

Owen Winn Grimes (b. 1801) m. Elvisa P. Watson

Maria Grimes (1802-1844) m. George E. Monroe

Phillip Grimes (1803-1820)

Sidney Smith Grimes (b. 1806) m. Mrs. Lydia Ann Gess McCann

Carlo Grimes

Martha Jane Grimes (b. 1808) m. James Milton Young

Elizabeth Grimes (b. 1812) m. Levi Barkley

Charles William Grimes

Fourth Generation

Mary "Polly" Grimes

b. June 8, 1794 in Fayette County

d. 1866 in Bourbon County

m. (1) Henry C. Clay, 1810 and (2) Benjamin Talbott, 1825

Children of Mary and Henry Clay:[7]
Charles Clay (1812-1840) unmarried
Nancy Clay (1815-1836) unmarried
Jane Clay (d. 1852) m. Aris Talbott
*Samuel H. Clay

John Grimes
b. February 14, 1796 in Fayette County
d. August 23, 1836
m. May 12, 1819, Rachel Waggoner (b. 1796) in Fayette
County

Children of John and Rachel:
James Grimes (1833-1852)
*Mary Grimes

Carlo Grimes
b. March 9, 1810 in Fayette County
d. 1883 in Lexington
m. June 7, 1838, Maria Louisa Talbott (b. 1818) in Bourbon
County

Children of Carlo and Maria Louisa:[8]
*Ara Jane "Jennie" Grimes
Willis T. Grimes (b. 1843)
Albert Grimes (b. 1846)
Talitha "Willy" Grimes (b. 1848)
*Charles P. Grimes
John W. Grimes (b. 1853)
Orrin H. Grimes (b. 1855)
Clarence Grimes (b. 1859)

Charles William Grimes
b. March 5, 1817 in Fayette County
d. March 12, 1886 in Fayette County
m. January 23, 1840, Mary Ann Embry (1819-1875) in Madison
County

Children of Charles W. and Mary Ann:[9]

Erasmus Darwin Grimes (1840-1911) m. Georgia Brewton

Joel Embry Grimes (b. 1842) m. Sallie A. Ballew

Charles O. Grimes (1844-c1866) not married

Martha Grimes (b. 1846) m. ___ Scott

Edwin R. Grimes (1847-1906) not married

Eusebius Grimes (b. 1848) not married

William Wallace Grimes (b. 1850) not married

Talton Grimes (b. 1852) not married

Jesse Embry Grimes (1853-1928) m. Annie Rachel Lindsay (1863-1936)

Orlando Talbott Grimes (1854-1929) m. Frances Amelia Callier

Mary Ann "Annie" Grimes (1856-c1931) m. John T. Denton

Ruth D. Grimes (1859-1937) m. (1) Dory Veal and (2) Robert White

Jennie P. Grimes (1861-1933) m. James McDonald

Fifth Generation

Ara Jane "Jennie" Grimes

b. 1842 in Clark County

m. October 3, 1865, *Henry C. "Harry" Clay* (b. 1839) in Clark County

Children of Jennie and Harry Clay:[10]

Ernest Clay

Samuel H. Clay

b. 1820

m. Julia Kennedy

Children of Samuel and Julia:[11]

Annie Clay

Frank Clay

Margaret Clay

Washington K. Clay (b. 1838)

Henry C. "Harry" Clay (b. 1839) m. *Ara Jane "Jennie" Grimes*, 1865, in Clark County

Charles G. Clay (b. 1845)

Mattie Clay (b. 1850)
B. J. Clay (b. 1852)
Samuel Clay (b. 1854)
William D. Clay (b. 1857)

Mary Grimes
b. 1825
m. c1844, James William Lindsay (b. 1822)

Children of Mary and James William Lindsay:[12]
John Lindsay (b. 1843)
William Lindsay (b. 1856)
Mary Lindsay (b. 1848)
Philip Lindsay (b. 1849)
Martha Jane Lindsay (1850-1925) m. *O'Connell McCuddy*
Elizabeth Lindsay (b. 1855)
Laura Lindsay (b. 1856) m. ___ Jones
Charles C. Lindsay (1857-1936) m. *Fannie Smitha* (1866-1921)
Jesse T. Lindsay b. 1864)
Anne Lindsay (b. 1865) m. Jess Grimes

Charles P. Grimes
b. 1851 in Clark County
m. Mary "Mollie" Lewis (b. 1857)

Children of Charles and Mary:
Clay Grimes (b. 1880)

D.
Grimes Mill
Chain of Title

December 3, 1782   James Nevill placed an entry for 250 acres on Boone Creek by virtue of a Treasury Warrant
Fayette County Entry Book 1, p. 27

February 22, 1788   Charles Morgan surveyed a 250-acre tract on Boone Creek for James Neavill; George Shortridge and Cornelius Ringo, chain carriers
Old Virginia Surveys, Volume 11, p. 341

March 3, 1788   James Neavill assigned the tract to Eli Cleveland
Old Virginia Surveys, Volume 11, p. 341

July 13, 1816   Grant for 250 acres issued to Eli Cleveland by the state of Kentucky, signed by Governor Isaac Shelby
Old Kentucky Grants, Volume 2, p.289

May 4, 1805   Eli and Mary Cleveland sold 60 acres and 30 poles on Boone Creek to John Winn Jr. and Charles Grimes, tenants in common (tract included the site where the mill would be built in 1807)
Fayette County Circuit Court Deed Book B, p. 335

October 1837   Charles Grimes' will probated, devising his "home residence and all the lands appertaining thereto in Clark and Fayette counties" (including the gristmill) to wife

Jane Grimes and sons Charles W. Grimes and Carlo Grimes, an undivided one-third interest to each
Fayette County Will Book N, p. 198

August 2, 1856

At Jane Grimes' death, Charles W. Grimes and Carlo Grimes each became one-half owners of the mill tract, as directed in Charles Grimes' will
Fayette County Will Book N, p. 198

March 23, 1873

Charles W. Grimes' one-half interest in the gristmill sold by a commissioner of the court at public auction to Henry C. Clay, son-in-law of Carlo Grimes (deed issued May 26, 1876)
Fayette County Deed Book 55, p. 584

August 10, 1885

A commissioner of the court sold the mill tract at public auction to Robert R. Stone, and the same day Stone deeded the property to Mary M. Grimes, wife of Charles P. Grimes (son of Carlo Grimes)
Fayette County Deed Book 74, p. 53

March 14, 1887

A commissioner of the court sold the mill tract at public auction to Robert R. Stone (deed issued June 8, 1887)
Fayette County Deed Book 78, p. 47

March 11, 1889

Robert R. and Elizabeth H. Stone sold the mill tract to Martha J. McCuddy
Fayette County Deed Book 83, p. 325

August 8, 1912

Martha J. McCuddy sold the mill tract to E. B. Wrenn and F. A. Bullock
Fayette County Deed Book 166, p. 90

August 30, 1913 | E. B. and M. E. Wrenn and F. A. and Grace Bullock sold the mill tract to Nannie J. Gaitskill
Fayette County Deed Book 171, p. 217

December 4, 1914 | Nannie J. and C. W. Gaitskill sold the mill tract to E. B. Wrenn and F. A. Bullock
Fayette County Deed Book 176, p. 404

November 29, 1915 | E. B. and Mary Wrenn and F. A. and Grace Bullock sold the mill tract to Allie B. Webb
Fayette County Deed Book 179, p. 587

September 23, 1916 | Allie B. and R. S. Webb sold the mill tract to C. C. Lindsay
Fayette County Deed Book 183, p. 42

January 11, 1921 | Charles C. and Fannie Lindsay sold two-thirds interest in the mill tract to George W. Kirby
Fayette County Deed Book 205, p. 383

March 25, 1922 | C. C. Lindsay sold his remaining one-third interest in the mill tract to George W. Kirby
Fayette County Deed Book 210, p. 267

November 20, 1923 | George W. and Lillie M. Kirby sold the mill tract to Annie M. Bowen
Fayette County Deed Book 221, p. 627

March 21, 1928 | Annie M. and Y. C. Bowen sold the mill tract to the Iroquois Realty Company (*current owner*)
Fayette County Deed Book 248, p. 497

E.
Peter Paul, Stonecutter

According to tradition, Peter Paul and his team of Irish stonemasons built Grimes Mill.

> The mill was built for Philip Grimes in 1803 by a crew of Irish builders and stone workers, captained by one Peter Paul.[1]

Although no contemporary records have been found to connect Peter Paul with Grimes Mill, he was a stone worker and was in the right place (Lexington) at about the right time (early 1800s) to be the builder. The tradition, however, raises more questions than it answers. For starters, it is fairly certain that the mill was built for Charles Grimes, not Phillip. Then, a more detailed version of the legend states that Grimes

> [sent] to New England for an Irish contractor and builder named Peter Paul, who came to Kentucky with a crew of thirty Irish stone workers.[2]

Paul came to Lexington in about 1802, the first year he appeared on the tax rolls for Fayette County. It is possible that he came out from Pennsylvania, where he still owned land the time of his death.[3] There is no indication that he came out at Grimes' bidding. Shortly after arriving in Lexington, Paul set up business on what is now Versailles Road, hung out his shingle, and placed a notice in the *Kentucky Gazette*:

> Peter Paul & Son, Stone Cutters From London, Now living on the Woodford road, Lexington, Respectfully inform their friends and the public at large that they carry on the Stone Cutting business in all its various branches, such as Tombs, Grave Stones of all sorts, Polished Marble Chimney Pieces, and Freestone Chimney Pieces, Safes to preserve Papers, Money, &c. from being destroyed in case of Fire.[4]

Paul's notice announced that he was a "stone cutter." He gave no indication that he was prepared to erect stone buildings. The stonecutter's trade—making stone products such as gravestones—differed from the stonemason's trade. Stonemasons were builders. They built houses, walls, bridges, and all sorts of structures out of stone. While there may have been considerable overlap in the two professions, each took care as to what they called themselves. The first city directory for Lexington, printed in 1806, listed eight men in the stone trades:

> William Palmateer, Stone-quarrier
> J. R. Shaw, Stone-cutter
> James Loney, Stone-mason
> Joseph Beatty, Stone-mason
> M. Rule, Stone-mason
> Warner Hawkins, Stone-mason
> Robert Russell, Stone-cutter
> Peter Paul, Stone-cutter[5]

The fact that Peter Paul identified himself as a stonecutter does not present a strong argument for him being a builder, though, of course, it does not rule it out either.[6] Also, Paul's announcement in the *Gazette* would seem to argue against the idea that he came to town "with a crew of thirty Irish stone workers." Such crews are associated with another historical tradition—the building of stone fences in the Bluegrass. The Irish were in Kentucky early, but large numbers of stoneworkers did not begin to arrive until the mid-1800s, the time of the potato famine in Ireland.[7]

While it is difficult to give up on such a vivid image as presented in the tradition, it has likewise been difficult to find concrete evidence to support it. To date, the author has been able to find only a single instance connecting Peter Paul and Charles Grimes in Fayette County records: when James Graves sold a tract of land on Boggs Fork to Charles Grimes. Graves gave Grimes a bond for $1,000 to guarantee that he would provide Grimes with "a good and sufficient deed." Peter Paul Jr. witnessed Graves' signature, as did Henry Clay. Paul's presence could have been merely a coincidence, as his home and business were not far from Henry Clay's law office.[8]

❀ ❀ ❀

Peter Paul quickly made a name for himself in Lexington and achieved some success—even notoriety—in his profession. In December of 1802, Paul purchased town lot No. 34. He paid 6 shillings for the property, which previously had sold for 20 pounds. The lot was bounded by Second, Market, Third, and Mill streets.[9]

In 1804, Paul took sixteen-year-old Francis Walker as an apprentice "to teach him the art & mystery of the stone cutting business." To have gotten an apprentice so quickly, Paul must have excelled in his profession and wasted no time establishing a local reputation.[10] The city directory indicates that he succeeded in spite of considerable competition in the field. His business address in 1802 was Versailles Road, in 1806 it was Short Street, and later Peter Paul & Son moved to Market Street. A contemporary of Paul's recalled those living on Market Street:

> Peter Paul & afterwards P. Paul & Son, had their
> Stone cutter's yard and small residence in from the
> street, a door or two above the Episcopal church.[11]

In 1818, Lexington's second city directory listed "Paul and Walters, Stone-Cutters" on Market Street.[12]

An anonymous letter to the *Gazette* by "Kentucky Farmer" slandered Paul and a number of other foreign-born craftsmen. The Farmer wrote, "I rejoice and approve of the attack made on those aliens," then continued in the same vein:

> I have no notion at all that we are to be taught and
> instructed by foreigners; that such fellows as Essex
> should pretend to take the lead in bookbinding, Paul
> in stone cutting.... All those improvements ought
> to be left to our own native born citizens....[13]

The fact that Paul was named may indicate that he was recognized as being in the top echelon of stoneworkers in Lexington. Paul and the others seem to have survived the attacks. The county awarded Paul a contract to provide the "sills to the Court house doors." He submitted a bill for 6 pounds, 7 shillings, 9 pence, which John Bradford was ordered to pay "if there is that much in his hands belonging to the County."[14] Paul had to take several of his clients to court to collect payment. He won a judgment against Jonathan Pew and Thomas Chamberlin for 20 pounds, 10 shillings, 7 pence, and another against Fielding Smith for $80.[15]

As Peter Paul and his son prospered in Lexington, they used some of their assets to acquire more property in the growing town. Peter Paul Jr. purchased a lot on Upper Street from Henry Clay for $250. Peter Sr. bought an adjoining lot at the same price. These transactions appear among the papers of Henry Clay.[16]

Peter Jr. purchased a lot on Market Street between Second and Mechanic. It was in the Transylvania University area and fronted on Gratz Park. In 1816, Paul built a house on the property, which would soon be surrounded by distinguished neighbors. The names of those living on the park included John Wesley Hunt, Thomas Pindell, Thomas Bodley, John Stark, Dr. Horace Holley of Transylvania, John McCalla, and Benjamin Gratz.[17]

The *Kentucky Reporter* carried a notice of the marriage of Peter Paul Sr.'s only daughter:

> In this town [Lexington], Mr. Hubbard B. Smith
> weds Sarah Paul, daughter of Mr. Peter Paul.

Smith went into the grocery business in Lexington in 1818. He advertised the sale of products—flour, corn, and bran—from the Steam Mill of Robert Huston & Co.[18]

Peter Paul had a brief but auspicious career in Lexington. When he made out his will, he held property in Pennsylvania, two town lots in Lexington, and several shares in the Madison Hemp and Flax Spinning Company.[19]

Peter Paul, the stonecutter, died in Lexington in 1822. He left his wife Sarah all of his estate and made provisions for dividing his property after her death.[20] In spite of his one time prominence in Fayette County, Paul is practically unknown here today. This may be due to several factors—the paucity of records for early Lexington, the short span of years he plied his trade in the city, and to his family later dying out or leaving the area. The one thing he is remembered for stems from the legend that he and his "team of thirty Irish stonemasons" built Grimes Mill.

Further Reading

Numerous published works can be consulted to get a basic understanding of mills and milling processes. For an introduction to how mills work, the following resources are ideal for the amount of detail they provide without weighing the reader down with technical jargon.

Marion Rawson, *Little Old Mills* (New York; 1935). Well-written book covering a multitude of mill types, which includes a lot of history and many drawings of mills and equipment.

David Macaulay, *Mill* (Boston; 1983). Macaulay, the artist, explains how mills work in a series of large annotated drawings that begin with selection of the mill site and continue through construction and operation of the mill.

Martha and Murray Zimiles, *Early American Mills* (New York; 1973). An outstanding collection of photographs, plans, and drawings of mills with history and explanatory text.

The Society for the Preservation of Old Mills (SPOOM) is an organization created to promote interest in milling. The society has a quarterly magazine, *Old Mill News*, and they publish new books and reprints of early books dealing with all aspects of milling. Several of their reprints will be useful for readers wishing to get into the details of mill construction and operation.

Oliver Evans, *The Young Mill-Wright & Miller's Guide* (Philadelphia; 1795). A classic publication by a major figure in the early U.S. milling industry, best known for his patents for the "mechanized mill."

James Leffel, *Construction of Mill Dams* (Springfield, OH; 1881). A primer on the different types of dams.

Fitz Water Wheel Co., *Fitz Steel Overshoot Water Wheel, Bulletin #70* (Hanover, PA; 1928). Although published to promote Fitz products, the bulletin describes many different types of water wheels and their practical application.

Benjamin Dedrick, *Practical Milling* (Chicago; 1924). A detailed description of all types of equipment and processes used in early and modern mills. Written at a technical level for industrial engineers.

While a number of states have extensive published material about their old mills, Kentucky is not one of them. The Commonwealth has made little effort to inventory or preserve its vanishing mills. From time to time, local newspapers carry stories about mills that once stood in their areas, but a compilation of these articles does not exist and would be difficult to undertake. County histories often contain brief descriptions of early mills and are worth seeking out. Several references are included here as examples:

Kathryn Owen, *Old Homes and Landmarks of Clark County, Kentucky* (Winchester; 1967), pp. 15, 24-25, 55.

Ann Bevins, *A History of Scott County as Told by Selected Buildings* (Georgetown; 1981), pp. 260-266.

H. E. Everman, *History of Bourbon County, 1785-1865* (Paris; 1977), pp. 8-11, 36-41.

For a description of early milling in Kentucky, it would be difficult to top the first-hand account of Ebenezer Hiram Stedman, papermaker, in Frances Dugan and Jacqueline Bull, editors, *Bluegrass Craftsman* (Lexington; 1952). This is the same Frances Smith Dugan (later Shine) who drew the sketch of Grimes Mill found in *Letters, A Quarterly Magazine Published by the University of Kentucky* (May 1928) 1:22.

The list of books and articles focusing specifically on milling in Kentucky is not long. One of the earliest articles described the various uses of millstones. William Webb, "Old Millstones of Kentucky," *Filson Club History Quarterly* (October 1935) 9:209.

Several individuals have collected extensive data and thoroughly documented various aspects of Kentucky's early milling industry. Nancy O'Malley, archeologist at the Cultural Resource Assessment Program, University of Kentucky, has completed a number of outstanding studies that will serve as examples for others in future investigations. Two of her reports deal with mills in the proximity of Grimes Mill.

Chris Amos and Nancy O'Malley, *Milling and Related Industry in the Boone Creek Drainage, Fayette and Clark Counties* (Lexington; 1991). This historical and archaeological investigation of Boggs Fork and the lower reaches of Boone Creek documents six mill and/or distillery sites, eight milling-related sites, and sixteen other historical sites. Includes a good general overview of early mill operation.

Nancy O'Malley, *Peter Evans' Mill, Nineteenth-Century Industry in Fayette County, Kentucky* (Lexington; 1999). This report describes an in-depth archaeological investigation and historical reconstruction of a nineteenth-century water-powered gristmill on Raven Run, which was located in what is now the Raven Run Nature Sanctuary.

Other writings by O'Malley on milling in Kentucky include *The Culture History and Archaeology of the McConnell Springs Natural and Historic Site* (Lexington; 1996) and *The Historic Milling Industry in the Fort Knox Military Reservation, Bullitt, Hardin and Meade Counties, Kentucky* (Lexington; 1996).

Charles Hockensmith, an archeologist with the Kentucky Heritage Council, has established himself as a national authority on millstones. He has conducted extensive investigations on millstone manufacturing in the U.S. and Europe. He has published reports describing a millstone quarry in Kentucky and the mills of Franklin County.

Charles Hockensmith and Larry Meadows, "Conglomerate Millstone Quarrying in the Knobs Region of Powell County, Kentucky, *Old Mill News* (Spring 1997 and Summer 1997), an in-depth study of a millstone quarry near Pilot Knob.

Charles Hockensmith, "The Stedman Mill Complex," *Old Mill News* (Fall 1995), an historical and archeological study of Hiram Stedman's paper mill.

Charles Hockensmith, "A. W. Macklin's Elkhorn Mills," *Old Mill News* (Winter 1999 and Spring 1999).

A very thorough archeological investigation of the mills at Shakertown, Pleasant Hill, has been published. The report describes the results of digs from 1975 to 1978. Donald Janzen, *The Shaker Mills on Shawnee Run* (Harrodsburg; 1981).

A considerable amount of historical and interpretive material on Mill Springs may be found in a brochure produced by the Army Corps of Engineers, *Mill Springs Mill* (Nashville; 1988).

One can only hope that the literature concerning Kentucky's mills and other early industries will continue to grow in the future. Much work remains to be done.

Notes

Preface

[1] The first Kentuckians used stone querns or stump-and-sapling mills to prepare their corn meal. The stone quern was a small, grinding mill consisting of a circular top stone that fit into a hollowed-out bottom stone, which held the grain. The top stone was usually turned by hand with the aid of a stick. The stump-and-sapling mill was a hand-powered mill made by attaching a pounding tool (usually the rounded end of a log) to a sapling or supple tree limb to give it a spring action. The base, which held the grain, was often a hollowed-out tree stump.

[2] Milling terms are defined in Appendix A. Gristmills were also powered by animals. Horse mills were fairly common in early Kentucky.

Chapter 1. Geographic and Historic Setting

[1] The Boone Creek Scenic Byway is a loop drive that follows portions of Athens-Boonesboro Road, Grimes Mill Road and McCalls Mill Road. Kentucky Transportation Cabinet pamphlet, "Kentucky's Scenic Byways" (Frankfort; n.d.).

Grimes Mill Road is one of the recommended tours in a recently published guide for Kentucky; an accompanying map places the Iroquois Hunt Club on the Clark County side of Boone Creek. William Kappele and Cora Kapple, *Scenic Driving in Kentucky* (Helena, MT; 2000), pp. 166-169.

[2] Enoch Smith deposition, July 5, 1805, *Charles Morgan vs. David Robinson*, 1805, Fayette County Circuit Court, Kentucky Land Trials, Record Book B:57. Enoch Smith, a neighbor of the Grimes family in Virginia, came to Kentucky in 1775, joining en route Richard Henderson's party bound for "Boonesborough."

The incident of Boone's capture by a Shawnee hunting party led by Captain Will occurred in December 1769. Boone and Stewart were forced to relinquish their horses and all the furs they had cached near their camp on Station Camp Creek (in present-day Estill County). Captain Will let the two men go, admonishing them, however, not to be caught in Kentucky again. Boone and Stewart followed the Shawnee and retook their horses, only to be captured once more. Captain Will showed remarkable patience, and even humor, in letting the men go a second time. John Faragher, *Daniel Boone, The Life and Legend of an American Pioneer* (New York; 1996), pp. 79-82.

In the same court case referred to above, Samuel Woods deposed that he knew of Boone's Creek in 1775, and it was then "known and called by that name." In his answer to Charles Morgan's complaint, David Robinson stated that "the first name of Boone's creek was Four mile creek, and he does not know when the change of name occurred." *Charles Morgan vs. David Robinson*, 1805, Fayette County Circuit Court, Kentucky Land Trials, Record Book B:22, 58.

[3] Stream and road names are spelled throughout as they appear on modern topographic maps.

[4] Boggs: Samuel Cassidy, *Story of a Log House* (Lexington; 1976). Boggs was born in New Castle County, Delaware. His historic home, Cave Spring, begun in the year 1792, still stands near the Athens-Walnut Hill Road. Robert's brother, James, settled in Madison County, Kentucky, and married Sarah ("Sary") Winn, daughter of Owen Winn.

Baughman: "Certificate Book of the Virginia Land Commission, 1779-1780," *Register of the Kentucky State Historical Society* (1923) 61:65; depositions of David Cooke, James Berry, and George Vallandingham, in *Boofman's heirs vs. James Hickman,* Fayette County Circuit Court, Kentucky Land Trials, Record Book A:604. This name is found under many different spellings, the most common of which are Boofman, Boffman, and Baughman. Ranck stated that the creek was named for "Captain John Boffman, who raised corn in that locality in 1776." George Ranck, *Boonesborough*, Filson Club Publications No. 16 (Louisville; 1901), p. 121.

[5] C. Frank Dunn, "Boone Station Site," *Register of the Kentucky Historical Society* (1943) 41:304 and (1946) 44:246.

Brief histories of the station are found in Nancy O'Malley, *Stockading Up, A Study of Pioneer Stations in the Inner Bluegrass Region of Kentucky* (Lexington; 1987) and Nancy O'Malley and Karen Hudson, *Cultural Resource Assessment of Boone Station State Park, Fayette County, Kentucky* (Lexington; 1993).

[6] William Perrin, editor, *History of Fayette County*, Kentucky (Chicago; 1882), p. 490.

[7] *Kentucky Gazette*, July 9, 1796. Other businesses were located at Cleveland's Landing. In one related to milling, John Gordon was selling millstones in assorted sizes from the Red River millstone quarry, which was located near Pilot Knob in present-day Powell County. *Kentucky Gazette*, June 13, 1799.

[8] By 1807, the road ran from Cleveland's Landing to Paris. Fayette County Order Book 1:499.

[9] John Phillips, *Historian's Guide to Loudoun County, Virginia* (Leesburg, VA; 1996), pp. 260, 338. Loudoun County, Virginia, was formed in 1757 from Fairfax County; Fairfax County was formed in 1742 from Prince William County.

[10] *Journals of the House of Burgesses of Virginia*, April 21, 1756, p. 374. In the fall of 1755 after Braddock's defeat, Phillip and Nicholas Grimes served in Captain Lewis Ellzey's company of Fairfax County militia. The company remained on duty for 50 days, except for Phillip Grimes, who was discharged after 15 days because of illness.

In a letter to George Washington on October 17, 1755, militia commander John Carlyle said of Ellzey's company, "they Are All Young healthy fellows, tolerable well mounted & Accouterred." W. W. Abbott, editor, *The Papers of George Washington, Colonial Series, Volume 2* (Charlottesville, VA; 1983), p. 122.

[11] Loudoun County (Virginia) Will Book A:144. Will signed August 5, 1765; probated June 1766.

[12] Margaret Hopkins, *Index to the Tithables of Loudoun County, Virginia* (Baltimore; 1991), pp. 31, 112.

[13] Record copied from *Kentucky Genealogist* (1960) 2:91. The entire record reads

> Philip Grimes of Loudoun. Debt with interest due 15 April 1777. £ 1.0.0. Removed to Kentucky about twenty years ago; then solvent. Enquire of Capt. William Stanhope of Fairfax.

When hostilities began in 1775, British property was confiscated, and Virginians refused to pay debts owed Loyalist merchants. The treaty following the Revolutionary War provided a mechanism for recovery of these debts, but it was not until 1800 that special agents in this country begin to follow up on the British claims.

Another claim returned to Virginia, this one for "debts due Jones' Executor," sought 663 pounds from "Philip Grymes [who] is alive and wealthy." It is not clear if this is the Phillip who went to Kentucky or another Phillip Grimes in Virginia. *Virginia Genealogist* (1966) 10:127.

[14] Neal Hammon, *Early Kentucky Land Records, 1773-1780* (Louisville; 1992), p. 150. The family name was often spelled "Grymes" in early Virginia and Kentucky records.

It may be helpful to summarize the steps involved in the land grant system of early Kentucky. Step #1 was the "warrant," a certificate that authorized a survey to be made. Warrants were purchased (treasury warrants), awarded for certain military service (military warrants), or awarded for actual settlement that met the conditions of Virginia law (settlement certificates and preemption warrants). Step #2 was the "entry," by which a claimant registered his intention to file for a grant. The entry was placed with the county surveyor at the land office. It gave the acreage, a description of the land to be surveyed, and the type of warrant. Step #3 was the "survey," the process of laying off a piece of ground that involved marking the lines and corners, recording the "metes and bounds," and preparing a plat or map of the tract. Step #4 was the "grant," also called a "patent." The warrant and survey were returned to the state capital (Richmond, Virginia prior to 1792), and the governor issued a grant. For additional detail, see Kandie Adkinson, "Kentucky Land Grant System," *Circuit Rider* (May-June 1990).

[15] Old Virginia Surveys, Volume 5:107, 11:325; Old Virginia Grants, Volume 5:109. Grimes later lost part of his Stoner Creek land when Enoch Smith, another Loudoun County neighbor, went to court to prevent the governor from issuing Grimes a grant for the 1,600-acre tract, the tract interfering with a survey of Smith's. The case was decided by the Kentucky Supreme Court in 1790, and Smith was allowed to carve 497 acres out of Grimes' claim. *Enoch Smith vs. Philip Grymes*, Kentucky Supreme Court, June Term, 1790, described in James Hughes, *A Report of the Causes Determined by the Late Supreme Court of the District of Kentucky and by the Court of Appeals in Which Titles to Land Were in Dispute,* 2d ed. (Cincinnati; 1869), pp. 35-37.

[16] Phillip Grimes was taxed for 1 white male between 16 and 21 years of age, 13 slaves, 8 horses, 12 cattle, and a "two-wheel carriage." James Grimes was listed as a tithable in the household of Phillip.

[17] Loudoun County families on Boone Creek included Winn, Lay, Dulin, Grigsby, Cockerill, Whaley, King, Ringo, Vallandingham and others. Fayette County tax lists, 1787; Marty Hiatt and Craig Scott, *Loudoun County, Virginia, Tithables, Volume 3* (Athens, GA; 1995).

The Grimes and Winn families were especially close. They would intermarry in Kentucky and exchanged land back in Virginia. By a deed dated July 22, 1800, Melinda Grimes [i.e., Valinda, widow of John] and Benjamin Grimes and wife Ann, all of Fayette County, sold to William Winn, also of Fayette County, a tract of 112 acres in Fairfax County, Virginia, on a branch of Accotink. Fayette County District Court Deed Book C:253.

[18] Deed dated May 1, 1798. Fayette County Burnt Records, Volume 5:52. The "Burnt Records" include many of Fayette County's early deed books

salvaged from a fire that destroyed county clerk Levi Todd's office in 1803.

[19] Old Virginia Surveys, Volume 7:284; Old Virginia Grants, Volume 13:319. Surveyed in 1786; grant issued in 1787. Grimes leased or bought the property well before the deed was recorded. He had been living there and paying taxes on the land since at least 1792, the first year that Fayette County listed real estate on the tax rolls.

[20] John was given half of Phillip's plantation without a formal deed. Fayette County tax rolls indicate that John paid the taxes on the property. In 1792, Phillip was assessed for 110 acres, and his son John was assessed for 110 acres. Records for subsequent years identify both tracts as part of Robert Boggs' land grant.

On August 20, 1798, three months after he obtained a deed from Boggs for 225 acres, Phillip conveyed by deed to his widowed daughter-in-law, Valinda Grimes, the 110-acre tract he had sold to his son John Grimes "in his lifetime." Fayette County Burnt Records, Volume 5:89.

[21] Fayette County Circuit Court, *Phillip Grimes' heirs vs. Charles Morgan heirs*, 1820. The court surmised that Grimes' actions had "probably taken the hint from the decision of the Old Supreme Court in the case of Smith vs. Grimes, which in all probability was founded, as appears by the original entries in this cause, on incorrect copies of the several entries involved."

[22] Fayette County Will Book B:53. Signed February 20, 1805; proved August 14, 1809. Phillip's will named seven sons, John (deceased), James, Avory, Benjamin, Stephen (deceased), Charles, and Phillip (deceased) and one daughter, Mary Payne. Phillip died February 20, 1806. Mary Grimes died before Phillip in 1796. Grimes family bible, copied in the *Louisville Courier Journal*, March 14, 1897.

It took a very long time to get Phillip's will proved. In April 1806, Benjamin Grimes petitioned the court to issue a summons to Daniel Lay to produce the deceased's will in court. When the will was then produced, Benjamin requested that proof of the will be continued until the next court. The case kept being continued until August 1809, when Benjamin finally removed his objection, and the will was proved. Fayette County Order Book 1:369, 438, 2:168.

[23] Grimes family bible, copied in the *Louisville Courier Journal*, March 14, 1897. This is confirmed by Fayette County tax records. Freeholders in Kentucky became taxpayers (tithables) when they reached age 21. Charles was not listed as a tithable in 1791, but he was in September 1792. His

tombstone states that he died on August 8, 1837, in his 67th year, thus at age 66.

There were two Charles Grimeses in the area in the early 1800s. The Grimes Mill proprietor always appeared in the records as simply "Charles Grimes." The second Charles appeared later on the scene and was designated as "Charles B. Grimes"; he married Elizabeth Boon in 1809 and operated a tavern in Bourbon County. Bourbon County Marriage Register, Book 2:41; *Kentucky Gazette*, July 24, 1818; Fayette County Deed Book 4:498.

Charles B. must have been closely related, as he purchased land near Charles' brothers, James and Benjamin. In 1811, Charles B. bought 14 ½ acres on a branch of Baughman Fork from Charles Lucus for $150. Fayette County Deed Book F:129.

The younger Charles was also referred to as "Charles B. Grimes Jr." Charles Grimes filed a lawsuit to collect from either George Clay or Charles B. Grimes Jr. a $60 debt that had been owed for two years. *Charles Grimes vs. George Clay*, Fayette County Circuit Court, 1820.

[24] Charles appeared on the Fayette County tax lists for 1792 and 1793. The lists for that end of Fayette County could not be located for the years 1794 and 1795. However, a 1795 deed stated that "Charles Grymes and Jane his wife of the City of Richmond, Virginia" sold Alexander Quarrier 1,200 acres of land on the Licking River in Kentucky. Kentucky Court of Appeals Deed Book A:279.

In a 1796 deed, "Charles Grymes and Jenny his wife of the City of Richmond, Virginia" sold John Hodgson 500 acres of land on the Eagle Creek in Kentucky. Jenny Grymes relinquished her dower before Richmond commissioners in March 1796. Fayette County District Court Deed Book 1:306

By June 1796, Charles was back in his father's household in Fayette County when the tax roll was taken. While Charles was not named on the tax rolls between 1796 and 1804, during this period Phillip was listed as "Phillip Grimes & Son." This "Son" was almost certainly Charles. The 1805 rolls have the same Grimes names as 1804 except that Phillip is missing, and there is an entry for "Capt. Charles Grimes & Father." Phillip wrote his will in 1805, so he may have been in poor health by then.

[25] Fayette County Order Book 1:45, 229, 419, 532, 533, 2:365, 372; Fayette County Guardian Book 1:155; Fayette County Marriage Records; G. Glenn Clift, *The "Cornstalk" Militia of Kentucky, 1792-1811* (Frankfort; 1957), p. 79; Fayette County Will Book B:53.

[26] *Betsy Grimes et al. by James Grimes, guardian vs. Charles Grimes,* Fayette County Circuit Court, 1811. Dinah and Harry both lived and appear to have been healthy adults. The plaintiffs sought $400 from Charles for the loss of Dinah.

[27] *Kentucky Gazette,* September 25, 1804. There are no deeds to Charles Grimes for property on Boggs Fork prior to this date; however, early land transfers often went unrecorded for many years. Fayette County tax lists do not show Charles assessed for any land on Boggs Fork at this time, an indication that he may not have owned the property he was offering for sale.

[28] The relationship is proved by John Winn's deposition taken at his house near Cross Plains, dated June 16, 1816: "Charles Grimes who intermarried with my Sister Jane Winn." The case involved Jane's right to part of her father Owen Winn's estate. *Charles Grimes vs. Jacob March,* Clark County Circuit Court, 1821.

[29] Old Virginia Surveys, Volume 2:245, 264, 268.

[30] Fayette County Deed Book B:335. John's activities are a little more difficult to follow than Charles', since there were two John Winns in Fayette County. John was referred to as "Jr." not because he was the son of John Sr., but rather to distinguish him from another John Winn in Fayette County, a first cousin who was usually designated as "Sr." Fortunately, the tax rolls of Fayette County make it possible to distinguish between these two men. John Winn Sr. was listed from 1791 through 1817 either under the name "John Winn" or "John Winn Sr." He can be identified by his land holdings on Elk Lick Creek, land originally granted to Eli Cleveland. John Winn Jr. was listed from 1800 through 1816 under numerous names. He was referred to as John Winn, Captain John Winn, Major John Winn, John Winn Jr., and once as Captain John Winn Jr. He can be identified by his land holdings on Boggs Fork, land originally granted to William Gillespie.

The two men can also be differentiated by their wives in some records. "John Winn Sr. and wife Mary" are identified in an 1815 deed (Fayette County Deed Book O:94), while another deed the same year mentions "John Winn and wife Susannah" (Fayette County Deed Book O:174).

[31] Fayette County Marriage Records, January 11, 1805. John appeared on the Fayette County list of tithables—those white males 21 years and older—for the first time in 1800. Assuming he turned 21 that year, he would have been born in 1779.

[32] Fayette County Will Book A:35. Signed September 8, 1805; proved January 1806. Owen Winn's will named his wife Mary and son John as

executors.   The will named two sons, John and Nathaniel, and nine daughters, Sary Boggs, Susannah Spurr, Elizabeth Vallandingham, Polly King (deceased), Jane Grimes, Anna Gess, Lydia Spurr, Doshia Young, and Barbary Winn.

Though he paid taxes on the property starting in 1800, John Winn did not receive a deed from his father for the 70 acres "on the cross plains." Land was often given or sold by parents to children, sometimes for several generations, without a deed being recorded with the court. Conveyance by will was usually as effective as a deed.

[33] G. Glenn Clift, *"Cornstalk" Militia of Kentucky, 1792-1811* (Frankfort; 1957), pp. 82, 205; Fayette County Order Book 1:354, 372, 403, 499, 2:492, 3:89; Fayette County Will Book A:389, C:365; Fayette County Guardian Book A:180. A number of other records refer simply to "John Winn" and cannot definitely be assigned to John Jr. or John Sr.

[34] Fayette County Will Book E:57, 58, 126. John appeared on the tax rolls for the last time in 1816; Susan was listed in 1817 and subsequent years. The sale of John's personal estate brought $727. In 1820, Susan Winn received her share of her husband's land: "The court have allotted to Susan Winn her dower in the land whereon said Susan Winn now lives." This land included 98 acres on Boggs Fork and 14 acres of "woodland." Fayette County Will Book E:356.

Since he left no will, we don't know if John had any children. There is evidence that he did. An 1822 deed conveyed land on the waters of Boone Creek from John Henry to several of the Winns, including "Susanna Winn and the heirs of John Winn, deceased." Fayette County Deed Book W:66.

Chapter 2. Charles Grimes Builds A Mill

[1] Article by John Gourlay, *Lexington Herald*, February 21, 1929.

[2] *Lexington Herald*, February 27, 1930, September 28, 1958, October 6, 1963, et al.; *The Chase Magazine,* January 1928, W. Fauntleroy Pursley, *Iroquois Hunt* (Lexington; 1955); J. Winston Coleman, *Historic Kentucky* (Lexington; 1967), p. 53; Betty Kerr, "National Register of Historic Places Inventory, Nomination Form," 1980.

[3] *Lexington Herald*, March 18, 1928.

[4] John Gourlay was secretary of the Iroquois Hunt Club at that time. Gourlay, who resided for a short time in Lexington (about 1925 to 1930), was general manager of the Superior Oil Corporation, a member of the Oil Men's Association, and an ardent foxhunter. R. L. Polk and Co., *Lexington City Directory*, 1923, 1925, 1928, 1930-31.

In 1929, Gourlay published an article in the 36th Annual of the National Foxhunters Association. Here he wrote that "Grimes employed an Irish contractor and builder from Philadelphia named Peter Paul who came from the east with a crew of 30 Irishmen to build a dam and mill race and the mill itself." Quoted in *Lexington Herald*, January 11, 1942.

[5] *Kentucky Gazette*, May 7, 1802.

[6] William Perrin, editor, *History of Fayette County, Kentucky* (Chicago; 1882), p. 489. At the time Perrin wrote this, the Grimes family still owned the mill.

[7] Fayette County Deed Book B:335. Eli Cleveland and his wife Mary sold John Winn Jr. and Charles Grimes, as tenants in common, a tract containing 60 acres and 30 poles. There are 160 poles in an acre, so 30 poles represents about one-fifth of an acre. It was soon recognized that the tract contained more than 60 acres. On the tax rolls, Grimes was assessed for 70 acres on Boone Creek. The area calculated after plotting the metes and bounds is approximately 75 acres.

The acreage listed in a deed was no guarantee of what the buyer was getting. That was controlled by the "metes and bounds" in association with the corners and boundaries marked on the ground. The actual acreage could be somewhat more or less than the amount stated in the deed. Winn and Grimes were fortunate in that their tract was larger than stated, being close to 75 acres.

[8] Fayette County Entry Book 1:27; Old Virginia Surveys, Volume 11:341; Old Kentucky Grants, Volume 2:289. Neavill's entry was made in 1782, the survey in 1788. Cleveland did not receive his grant for the property until 1816. The plat accompanying the survey indicates that Cleveland's tract was situated on the west side of Boone Creek and the south side of Boggs Fork.

[9] Fayette County Order Book 1:277.

[10] "An Act to reduce into one, the several acts concerning Mill-Dams and other obstructions in Water Courses, 1797," in William Littell, *A Digest of the Statute Law of Kentucky, Volume 1* (Frankfort; 1822), pp. 409-413.

[11] Ibid.

[12] Fayette County Order Book 1:290, 310.

[13] Fayette County Order Book 1:320.

[14] Fayette County Order Book 1:331.

[15] William Littell, *A Digest of the Statute Law of Kentucky, Volume 1* (Frankfort; 1822), pp. 409-413.

[16] Fayette County Order Book 1:444.

[17] Fayette County Order Book 1:451, 461.

[18] Fayette County Order Book 2:293. The twelve jurors were all neighbors of Winn and Grimes in Fayette County (see Appendix B).

Two dates appeared in the jury's report. May 4, 1807, was given as the date the jurors met on Boone Creek, and April 4, 1807, was given as the date the jurors signed the report. One of the dates is obviously in error. Since their report was returned to court on April 13, the jury must have met on April 4, not May 4.

[19] Fayette County Order Book 1:528.

[20] The deed from Cleveland to Winn and Grimes conveyed the land "together with all ways, woods, water courses, mines, minerals, quarries and all and every of its appurtenances of every kind...." The deed does not mention a mill but does refer to quarries. "Ways, woods, water courses" are frequently listed as appurtenances in deeds, but "mines, minerals, quarries" is a very unusual reference that would indicate that one or more of the latter was present on the site in 1805. This quarry could have supplied stone for Phillip Grimes but that seems unlikely. Tax records and deeds indicate that Phillip never owned the property. And Charles Grimes probably did not acquire the property prior to his 1805 deed, since the land appeared on his Fayette County tax assessment for the first time in the 1806 rolls. Fayette County Circuit Court Deed Book B:335.

[21] Deed of sale for 129 acres on Boggs Fork from James Hawkins to James Grimes, dated March 30, 1812. Fayette County Deed Book F:453.

Chapter 3. Mill Construction: An Architectural Review

[1] The guidelines followed for documenting Grimes Mill structures were obtained from Harley McKee, *Recording Historic Buildings* (Washington, D.C.; 1970) and "Production Notes" of the Historic American Buildings Survey (www.cr.nps.gov/habshaer).

[2] To calculate the theoretical horsepower for a site, multiply the head (measured in feet) times the flow rate of water (measured in cubic feet per minute) and divide the product by 529. Thus, a site with a head of 18 feet and a flow of 1,000 cubic feet per minute has a theoretical horsepower of 34. Multiplying the theoretical horsepower times the efficiency of the water wheel gives the usable horsepower.

[3] The stone used in the dam construction consists of large blocks of Kentucky River Marble and smaller blocks of Tyrone Limestone; the

rubble is mostly Tyrone Limestone. See the "Gristmill" section for a description of these stones.

[4] *Lexington Herald*, February 21, 1929.

[5] Fayette County Deed Book 38:142.

[6] Garland Dever, Kentucky Geological Survey, provided detailed information about the geological formations on Boone Creek and identification of the stone used in the mill and dam construction. Dr. Dever also located the small hillside quarry in the Tyrone Limestone on the north side of Grimes Mill Road. Other data were taken from the U.S.G.S. 7.5 Minute Geological Map, Ford Quadrangle.

The techniques of obtaining and dressing building stone in the late eighteenth-early nineteenth century are described in Harley McKee, "Early Ways of Quarrying and Working Stone in the United States," *Bulletin of the Association for Preservation Technology* (1971) 3:44. For two excellent essays on stone construction methods, see Carolyn Murray Wooley, "Kentucky's Early Stone Homes," *Antiques* (March 1974) 592, and Clay Lancaster, "Chapter 3—Stone Construction," *Antebellum Architecture in Kentucky* (Lexington; 1991), p. 45.

[7] *Lexington Herald*-Leader, November 4, 1962.

[8] One of these sketches was done by Frances Smith, "Sketch—Grimes Mill," *Letters, A Quarterly Magazine Published by the University of Kentucky* (May 1928) 1:22 and the other by Howard E. Smith, 1934, Iroquois Hunt Club collection. The photograph belongs to David and Cherry Fleischer.

[9] See for example, the mill layout in Oliver Evans, *The Young Mill-Wright & Miller's Guide* (Philadelphia; 1795), p. 74 and Plate VII.

According to Ted Hazen, the basement fireplace may have been used for the miller's branding irons that were needed for marking the flour barrels with the name and weight.

[10] Mortice-and-tenon joints are a method of fastening wood pieces together, where a slot is cut in the end of one piece (the "mortice") to receive a corresponding projection (the "tenon") at the end of another piece. The joint was held in place by inserting a wooden peg into a hole drilled through the joint.

For a description of early wood construction techniques and terms, see Norman Isham's *Early American Houses* (Boston; 1928) and *A Glossary of Colonial Architectural Terms* (Boston; 1939).

[11] Timbers used in the mill's beams and posts vary from 11 to 13 inches on a side. While several newspaper articles refer to these framing timbers as

oak, wood samples from a beam and a joist were identified by Jim Ringe of the Forestry Department, University of Kentucky, as American chestnut, *Castenea dentata*. This raises more questions, however, since according to Rob Paratley, University of Kentucky Herbarium, chestnut did not grow in the inner Bluegrass region. The tree was not reported in a study of early Bluegrass vegetation. (Julian Campbell, "Present and Presettlement Forest Conditions in the Inner Bluegrass of Kentucky," Ph.D. dissertation, University of Kentucky, 1980.) Chestnut was plentiful in the Knobs and eastern Kentucky and may have been floated down the Kentucky River to be used in flatboat construction. One finds it difficult to explain why the mill builders would pass up the massive oaks and walnuts that must have grown in the Boone Creek gorge near the mill site and were essentially free for the taking. It is especially difficult in view of the alternative, which would have been to haul timbers up from the river over very difficult ground, a costly and labor-intensive process. It seems unlikely that they would do so without good reason. One possible explanation is that seasoned chestnut logs may have been available (at Cleveland's boatyard, for example) and may have been a better choice for framing than unseasoned oak.

The major species growing in the Boone Creek gorge now are sugar maple (*Acer saccharum*), black walnut (*Juglans nigra*), American beech (*Fagus grandifolia*), chinquapin oak (*Quercus muehlengergii*), white oak (*Q. alba*), bur oak (*Q. macrocarpa*), swamp white oak (Q. bicolor), yellow buckeye (*Aesculus octandra*), and shagbark hickory (Carya ovata). The same species were common at the time of settlement. Op. cit.

[12] This type of roof system is described in Hugh Morrison, *Early American Architecture* (New York; 1952), pp. 26, 36.

[13] Fitz Water Wheel Co., *Bulletin No. 70, Fitz Steel Overshoot Water Wheels* (Hanover, PA; 1928).

[14] *Lexington Herald*, January 11, 1942.

[15] Conglomerate is a pebble-filled sedimentary rock commonly used for millstones. Its hardness comes from the quartz pebbles. The millstone quarry near Pilot Knob was described by Charles Hockensmith and Larry Meadows, "Conglomerate Millstone Quarrying in the Knobs Region of Powell County, Kentucky, *Old Mill News* (Spring 1997 and Summer 1997).

[16] U.S. Manufacturers Census, Fayette County, 1870.

[17] The author is indebted to Ted Hazen, an experienced millwright and mill interpreter, for his assistance in the sections dealing with milling-related equipment and operations. Upon examining the measured drawings,

Hazen offered the suggestion that Grimes Mill may have had two water wheels at one time. His conjecture is based on the fact that there were two doors on the rear wall opening into the wheel pit. One of the doors centers on the existing metal wheel; the other door has been filled in with stone, but could have centered on another wheel. There is sufficient room for a second wheel in the pit. No other physical evidence for a second wheel is available at the time, but it is an intriguing idea.

[18] Oliver Evans, *The Young Mill-Wright & Miller's Guide* (Philadelphia; 1795). Oliver Evans (1755-1819) patented his mill improvements for which he originally charged users $40 per millstone. His inventions were widely copied, and he had a difficult time collecting his fee. Evans' patents were a tremendous improvement not only in efficiency but also in the amount of labor involved in the manufacture of flour. One man literally could operate his mill. Contrast that with the previous process:

> If the grain be brought to the Mill by land carriage, the Miller took it on his back, a sack generally three bushels, carried it up one story by stair steps, emptied it in a tub holding four bushels, this tub was hoisted by a jack moved by the power of the Mill which required one man below and another above to attend to it, when the tub was moved by hand to the granary, and emptied. All this required strong men. From the granary it was moved by hand to the hopper of the rolling screen, from the rolling screen by hand to the Millstone hopper, and as ground it fell in a large trough, retaining its moisture, from thence it was with shovels put into the hoist tubs which employed two men to attend, one below, the other above, and it was emptied in large heaps on the Meal loft, and spread by shovels, and raked with rakes, to dry and cool it, but this necessary operation could not be done effectually, by all this heavy labour. It was then heaped up over the bolting hopper, which required constant attendance, day and night, and which would be frequently overfed, and cause the flour to pass off with the bran, at other times let run empty, when the specks of fine bran passed through the cloth, which with the great quantity of dirt constantly mixing with the meal from the dirty feet of every one who trampled in it, trailing it over the whole Mill and wasting much, caused great part [of the flour] to be condemned, for people did not even then like to eat dirt, if they could see it. After it was bolted it required much labour

to mix the richest and poorest parts together, to form the
standard quality. This lazy millers would always neglect,
and great part would be scrapped or condemned, while
others was [*sic*] above the standard.

Greville Bathe and Dorothy Bathe, *Oliver Evans, A Chronicle of Early
American Engineering* (Philadelphia; 1935), p. 12.

Evans would have been well known in Lexington at this time. In
1806, Luther Stephens began construction of the Lexington Steam Mill.
His mill was driven by one of Oliver Evans' steam engines and employed
the roller mill process. Stephens, a gifted engineer himself, designed an
improvement to the steam engine, a rotary valve that Evans incorporated in
later models. The Lexington Steam Mill went into operation in early
October 1809, the first steam-powered roller mill constructed in America.
Op. cit., pp. 141-142, 161; *Kentucky Gazette*, October 16, 1809.

Chapter 4. Early Years, 1807-1837

[1] Fayette County Order Book 1:528. Petition dated April 10, 1808.
William Cotton was Charles Grimes' neighbor to the west; the stone
meeting house has not been identified.

[2] Fayette County Order Book 2:25, 32, 47, 50. Cleveland and Poindexter
were summoned to court to voice any objections they might have.
Cleveland, whose warehouse was the object of Charles Grimes' road, gave
his consent. Poindexter, whose property adjoined Grimes, objected to the
road crossing his land. Sheriff John Morton empanelled a jury from the
neighborhood to view the road on August 22, 1808.

The jury found that the road would cross 700 yards of Poindexter's
land and awarded him ten dollars in damages, to be paid by Grimes. The
road was established by the court on October 10, 1808. Charles Grimes
was appointed overseer the same day. Poindexter had to sue Grimes to
collect the damages awarded him by the court. Fayette County Order
Book 2:250.

[3] Clark County Order Book 4:257. Petition dated July 1808.

[4] Clark County Order Book 4:277. Road established October 1808.

[5] The road down to Boone Creek must have been a hair-raising ride. The
Clark County side of the creek near Rogers Mill is lined with formidable-
looking cliffs, with no obvious route of descent. One of the road orders
states that Graham Hazelrigg, Daniel Barkley, John Morton, and Richard
Hickman were to mark a new road from Germantown to the county line at

Boone Creek, to intersect the creek "a half mile below Rogers mill."
According to their report, the road was to run

> along a ridge crossing Tolberts land to a red oak in Bartletts
> line, thence with his line to his gate, thence along his lane to
> the clift of Boons Creek and down the clift to Boons Creek.

Clark County Order Book 4:50.
The origin of the Germantown name is uncertain. It could have come
from the Revolutionary War battle of the same name or from the German
settlers in the area, such as the Heronimous family. First mentioned in a
road order in 1805, Germantown was a long-time precinct name and the
village was shown on the Clark County map of 1877. D. G. Beers and J.
Lanagan, *Atlas of Bourbon, Clark, Fayette, Jessamine and Woodford
Counties, Kentucky* (Philadelphia; 1877).

[6] Clark County Order Book 4:324. Petition dated July 1809.

[7] Heronimous' warehouse was established by the Kentucky legislature on
February 23, 1808. It was located on Henry Heronimous' land. Mary
Verhoeff, *The Kentucky River Navigation* (Louisville; 1917), pp. 231-232.

Johann Frantz (John Francis) Hieronymus was born in Vienna,
Austria, and immigrated to Philadelphia in 1747. His son Henry came to
Clark County from Loudoun County, Virginia, in about 1804. John
Francis came out sometime later. The family name appears under
numerous spellings in county records. Ben Hieronymus and R. Dean
Heironymus, *The Hieronymus Story*, 1985 (Baltimore; 1985), pp. 101-114.

[8] An act to establish Inspections of Flour and Hemp, 1795, in William
Littell, *A Digest of the Statute Law of Kentucky, Volume 1* (Frankfort;
1822), pp. 443-450. Barrels or "casks" had to be constructed in accordance
with strict standards. They were to be made of seasoned wood with staves
27 inches long and heads 17 ½ inches in diameter, tightened with 10 hoops
using 4 nails in each "chime hoop" and 3 nails in each "bilge hoop."

[9] *Kentucky Gazette*, July 9, 1796. Later operated as Rogers Mill.

[10] Deposition of Dennis Bradley in *Evan Francis vs. Benjamin Grimes and
John Hendley*, Fayette County Circuit Court, 1810.

[11] *Kentucky Gazette*, January 24, 1804. McCall offered his "merchant
mill" and distillery "for sale or rent" in 1810. *Kentucky Gazette*, August 7,
1810.

[12] With much greater cost and effort, one could go up the Ohio River to
Pittsburgh, but that city, west of the continental divide itself, was seeking
western markets for its own produce.

[13] Cleveland's, Bush's and Holder's warehouses were established in 1792, Jacks Creek and Stone's in 1799, and Heronimous' in 1808. Mary Verhoeff, *The Kentucky River Navigation* (Louisville; 1917), pp. 231-232.

[14] These boats followed a similar design, of which the one below is typical:

> [S]pecifications called for gunwales "fifty feet long and six inches square, the bottom planks two inches thick, twelve boards to be put across the boat, the side planks to be one and one-half inches thick. The stanchions or studs to be three by six, five feet high and five to a side. The boats to be finished in a workman-ship-like manner, to be pinned with seasoned white oak pins and bored, and the sides to be five feet high and the whole to be of oak timber." This was the structural description of the "Kentucky boat." A stout cabin, a pair of ornamental deer horns, a pair of side sweeps, and a long steering oar topped off the equipment.

Thomas Clark, *The Kentucky* (Lexington; 1969), p. 69.

[15] "I have an Orlean Boat for sale, 45 feet long & 14 feet wide, strong & well built, with 4 oars, cable, &c. It lies at Fulgerson's [Fulkerson's] ferry on the Kentucky river. For terms apply to the subscriber near the Cross-Plains, or the printer hereof. Benjamin Grimes." *Kentucky Gazette*, May 7, 1802.

Benjamin almost got into the milling business before his brother Charles. In 1805, Benjamin Grimes and John Hendley purchased Evan Francis' merchant gristmill, sawmill, and distillery on Boone Creek. Each was to pay Francis 1,125 pounds. The deal fell through in April 1805, on the day the contract was to be signed. They all met at Hendley's house at Cross Plains to sign the final papers, when one of Hendley's servants rushed in hollering, "The mill has fell in, the mill has fell in." He had just come from the mill where one of the walls had collapsed. Hendley refused to sign the contract on the grounds that Francis could not provide clear title to the property and would not give them a bond to guarantee the title. Francis sued them for breach of contract. Deposition of Dennis Bradley in *Evan Francis vs. Benjamin Grimes and John Hendley*, Fayette County Circuit Court, 1810.

Benjamin finally did get into the mill business in Jessamine County. In 1812, he leased William Shreve's gristmill on Hickman Creek. The business must not have been a complete success, since in 1821 Shreve leased the mill to his son-in-law, William Boyce. Billy Bower, *Mills, Murders and More in Early Days of Jessamine County, Kentucky* (Nicholasville; 1998), p. 2.

[16] *Kentucky Gazette*, August 25, 1802.

[17] G. Glenn Clift, *Remember the Raisin!* (Frankfort; 1961), pp. 142, 225. In the battle at Frenchtown on the River Raisin, south of Detroit, Bledsoe and Grimes were captured, and the former company commander, John Edmiston, was killed. Adam Winn and Thomas Winn Jr. were also in the company. All of these men were from the Athens-Boone Creek area. After the battle of Frenchtown, the British allowed their Indian allies to massacre many of the prisoners. The resulting outrage gave rise to the battle cry "Remember the Raisin" and helped fuel the ultimate American victory.

In 1818, Henry Clay filed with the federal government "John Grimes' petition for pay for a gun &c." His petition was unsuccessful. James Hopkins, editor, *The Papers of Henry Clay, Volume 2* (Lexington; 1959), p. 674.

Many other Grimeses from Kentucky served in the War of 1812, including the following who may have belonged to Phillip Grimes' branch of the family: Avory, three Johns, two Jameses, Thomas, and Willis. State of Kentucky, *Report of the Adjutant General of the State of Kentucky, Soldiers of the War of 1812* (Frankfort; 1891).

[18] John Filson, "Map of Kentucke," 1784; *Kentucky Gazette*, January 1, 1791, February 11, 1797; Old Virginia Grants, Volume 11:302; Fayette County Order Book 3:160, 4:274. Sulphur Well Road today ends at Boone Creek, just below the three forks. At one time, the road may have crossed Boone Creek and continued east to intersect Combs Ferry Road.

[19] Clark County Order Book 2:319, 336. Robinson's Mill was established by the Clark County court in October 1799.

Charles Morgan later sued David Robinson, William's brother, over property boundaries. Morgan and the two Robinsons held grants for adjoining (and overlapping) tracts on Boone Creek. The court decided in Morgan's favor in 1805. *Charles Morgan vs. David Robinson*, Fayette County Circuit Court, Kentucky Land Trials, Record Book B:1.

[20] Fayette County Order Book 1:163, 229; *Kentucky Gazette*, January 24, 1804. McCall's mill seat on Boggs Fork was established in 1804. He put his mills up for sale in 1810:

> For Sale or Rent, My Merchant mill, Saw mill, Distillery and Farm at Oak Ridge. This property is well situated for business, in Fayette county, near the Kentucky river. Or I will sell or rent the Harrogate watering place, with the mills attached to it, or either separately. This last place is well calculated for a school, or schools, both for female and male

education, having separate buildings suitable for both, and being in a fine neighbourhood, where such schools are much wanting. For terms, apply to John M'Call, Harrogate.

Kentucky Gazette, August 7, 1810.

A few years ago, a millstone was found near the three forks of Boone Creek by Debbie Young, whose husband farms the area that includes several mill sites. She stated that the millstone was "pebbly," which may indicate a conglomerate stone of the type manufactured at the Red River millstone quarry near Pilot Knob in Powell County. The stone could have come from the mills of Morgan, Robinson, or McCall.

[21] Fayette County District Court Deed Book C:338; Clark County Deed Book 10:51; Clark County Will Book 1:59. The first reference to this mill is found in the *Kentucky Gazette* on July 27, 1793. Numerous documents state explicitly that Hazelrigg's Mills were in Clark County. For example, a deed dated September 10, 1796, refers to

> a certain tract of Land in Clark County on Boons Creek containing Seventy Six Acres wherein the mill commonly known by the name of Hazelriggs Mill stands.

Fayette County District Court Deed Book A:55.

An 1800 deed, Niblack to McCall, describes one of the corners of the property being at "the Edge of Francis Mill dam" on Boone Creek. (Fayette County District Court Deed Book C:191) When plotted, this corner is found to lie about one-fourth of a mile below the Athens-Boonesboro Road.

[22] Clark County Order Book 2:251, 256. Beatty's petition was dated August 1798; it was quashed by the court in October 1798.

[23] *Kentucky Gazette*, November 10, 1806; Fayette County Order Book 2:35. William McCall advertised that his fulling mill would take wheat, corn, rye, and hemp in payment.

> The subscriber having erected a Fulling Mill on Boon's Creek, one mile from the Cross-Plains, and ten from Lexington; which is now in complete order and having learned the Fulling Business, in all its various branches, with one of the first workmen in Pennsylvania, and also worked a mill of his own in that State upwards of twenty years, flatters himself that he is capable of Dying and Dressing Cloth (perhaps) as well as any other in the State of Kentucky, and on as cheap terms. He therefore solicits a share of the public

patronage; assures them his best exertions shall not be wanted to render complete satisfaction to accommodate distant customers. Cloth for dressing will be received at T. & R. Barr's, merchant in Lexington, and at Mr. Posten, in Winchester, where he will attend on Mondays of every court week and return the Cloth Dressed agreeable to directions, on the next courts. Wheat, Corn, Rye, Hemp, Pork &c will be received in payment at the market prices. William M'Call.

An 1808 road order for William McCall's mill road gives valuable information about both of the McCalls' mills:

The report of the commissioners who were appointed to view the road petitioned for by William McCall was returned at last court and a summons issued to James Hickman, one of the proprietors of the land thru which said road will run, was returned [and] executed. The other proprietors of the land thru which said road will run gave their consent to its being opened as reported by the Commissioners except Hezekiah Harrison who is Guardian to the Heirs of David Gillespie who also consents to its being opened upon the following conditions that it will run along the line of the land of said Gillespies Heirs only taking a small part of a hill. The agents of said Hickman also appeared in Court a[nd] gave his consent to the opening said road. It is thereupon ordered that said report be recorded and that said road be established accordingly which report is as follows to wit:

Fayette County [*illegible*] Pursuant to an order of the County Court of Fayette made at the last October term upon the application of William McCall appointing the subscribers to view the ground beginning at William McCalls fulling mill, Saw and Grist mills from thence to John McCalls Grist mill along which a road is proposed to be established or conducted and report thereon. The subscribers being first duly sworn according to a certificate of Leonard K Bradley esq. a Justice of the peace for the County aforesaid hereto annexed and in obedience to the order aforesaid have went upon the ground along which such road is proposed to be conducted and inquired into the conveniences and inconveniences which will result as well to individuals as to the publick if such way shall be opened and report that a road beginning at William McCalls mills and running through [illegible] corner of said McCalls orchard field to it strike John Muirs line and thence along the line of said Muir and McCall untill it nearly strikes Muirs corner leaving sufficient room at said corner or angle for an easy passage of Waggons, thence along the line between said Muir and Frederick Nichols to the corner between Frederick Nichols and James Hickman Senior, thence along the line between Frederick Nichols and James Hickman Senior & John Laughlin to it strikes the Winchester road leading from the Cross plains [Athens], thence along said road to it strikes the mouth of the Widdow Parrishes lane, thence along said lane and on the line between David Walls and the Heirs of David Gillespie to it strikes the land of the Heirs of said Gillespie, thence through a small part of said Gillespies land to it strikes land of John McCall, thence through said McCalls land to it strikes boons creek a few pearches below said McCalls mill, would under all the circumstances of the case be the nearest and best way between the said mills by which a road could be laid out, that the said road would be of considerable utility as well to the owners of the land through which it passes and to the neighbourhood as to the publick generally, in this respect that the publick would have better access to said mills which are valuable establishments and usefull to a great part of the County and the subscribers are further of opinion that the said roads laid out in the manner aforesaid would produce no inconveniences to the private individuals or the publick generally, all which is respectfully subscribed to the worshipfull the Justices of the County aforesaid. Given under our hand and seals this eighth day of December one thousand eight hundred and seven.

    [signed] Thaddeus Dulin
            Randell Noe
            Samuel Boone

That John Muir, Frederick Nichols, John Laughlin, David Watts & John McCall have agreed that the aforesaid road as mentioned in this report and land onto should be conducted and established is certified by us this 11th day of January 1808.

    [signed] Thaddeus Dulin

Randell Noe
Samuel Boone Sr.

Fayette County Order Book 2: 35-37.

[24] *Kentucky Gazette*, February 16, 1793, April 25, 1795, April 9 and July 9, 1796. Eli Cleveland had several business ventures on his place near the mouth of Boone Creek. In 1793, he announced in the *Kentucky Gazette* that his "hemp mill is now operating." His gristmill on Boone Creek was evidently a merchant mill, for he advertised flour for sale in 1795. In April 1796, Cleveland wrote a letter to the editor regarding the burning of his mills.

> Mr. Bradford, Whereas there are diverse reports propagated by my enemies concerning the burning of my mills, it appears from their behavior and language that they would willingly make the public believe that some innocent person was the cause, and have gone so far as to say I burnt them myself, which reports are intended to cloak their own villany. Some of them have so far declared their malice against me as to wish I had been burnt with them. This can be proven. I take this method through the channel of your paper to inform the public of the circumstances of their being burnt.

> They were burnt on the 27th of March in the night, just before the moon had risen. I am able to prove there was not the least spark of fire any where about them [the mills] that evening. There were three tracks of persons discovered by a young man who lived at my mills. They came a private way by the mill dam. They had about twenty or thirty yards to wade up the side of the dam, where the water was waist deep. The track came and went the same way. No person ever attempted to pass that way from the first raising of the dam, unless the water was so low that the mill could not grind, which was very seldom. There was the print of the breech of a gun to be seen very plain in the mud, where it is supposed they pulled off their shoes to wade. The young man sent me word concerning the discovery he had made, upon which I took some persons with me, and we found every thing as above related. One of the tracks appears to be a boy's of about fifteen years old, and his feet bare. The other two were men, and had shoes on. They came and went

the same course the tracks went when my hemp was formerly burnt.

My mills were judged to be worth three thousand pounds; nay, I was offered that money for them and one acre of land they stood on. I lost about two hundred pounds worth of grain, flower and hemp in them, &c &c &c. Eli Cleveland

In July of that year, Cleveland put his mills up for sale. His ad in the *Gazette* gave additional details about his businesses:

For Sale, Four Hundred Acres Of Land, Including my Mills, Warehouse, Ferry, Boat-yard, Orchards, Meadows, &c. Great part of the land is first rate. There is belonging to the mills about two thousand weight of wrought iron proper for merchant business. The walls of the lower story of the mill-house is sound and as high as the mill-house. The water wheels have received little or no damage by the fire; and cogs and rounds well seasoned are ready. The race is planked at the [illegible] and walled with stone on both sides, and the dam perhaps the best in the state, and the stream equal to any. The saw mill is now running and in good order, and the water may be put to the grist mill wheels any minute. The grist mills may be set to running in four weeks. Beam, chains and scales well ironed for the purpose of weighing tobacco; and beam, chains, weights and iron for scales for weighing flour.

Boats may come up from the river to the mills in high water, the whole beautifully situated for merchant business, at the mouth of Boon's creek; and may be inclosed with about 300 pannels of fence. Waggons may pass to and from the landing with such loads as can be carried on any other roads.

As I am determined to sell, I will give a credit of one or two years for the greatest part of the purchase money; and if I cannot get the value, will take the best price offered and make an indisputable title. For terms apply to the subscriber near the premises. Eli Cleveland.

Cleveland sold his mills to John Fowler and Hugh McIlvain in 1797, who in turn sold to Jeremiah and Joseph Rogers in 1801. The latter had to sue Cleveland to obtain a deed to the property. *Jeremiah and Joseph Rogers vs. Eli Cleveland*, Fayette County Circuit Court, 1815.

In 1811, Jeremiah Rogers petitioned the court for a gristmill on Boone Creek, which suggests that the mill had gone out of operation for a period or that Rogers wanted to move or enlarge his dam or add another mill to his complex. Fayette County Order Book 2:388.

[25] Fayette County Deed Book F:453, S:460. Deeds dated March 30, 1812, and January 30, 1819, respectively.

[26] William Perrin, editor, *History of Fayette County, Kentucky* (Chicago; 1882), p. 489. The Owen Winn mill was from a later date than the others. According to Perrin:

> A small distillery was built near Athens. The building was originally put up in 1845, by Owen Winn, for a mill. This was burned about 1866; and in 1868, a distillery was built on the site by Adams & Devore. It was operated by them until 1876, and afterward by Poindexter & Pettitt, and then discontinued. It is now [1882] used for a tobacco barn.

Ibid., p. 212. Owen D. Winn, age 44, was listed in the 1850 U.S. Population Census, Fayette County, living in the Boone Creek neighborhood.

[27] Fayette County Order Book 1:185, 385, 403. Duncan's petition was dated 1804. Christian's mill was established in 1806. The jury returned the following report on William Christian's petition for erecting a gristmill:

> We of the Jury having been sworn agreeable to law and writ of Ad Quod damnum from the worshipful County Court of Fayette to the Sheriff of said County directed, and being on the lands of William Christian on Boffmans fork of Boon creek where said Christian proposes to erect a dam for the purpose of turning a grist mill do upon our oaths report & Say That we think said Christian may erect a dam across said Creek from a hickory and sugartree on the most eastwardly side to a sugar and white oak tree on the westwardly side, seven feet high, will not flow nor injure no one except one acre on the opposite bank belonging to Thomas Frank, which one acre Beginning at the sugar & white oak trees at the end of the dam & running up and down the said creek one hundred and five feet, thence at right angles from each end of said line so far out as to include one acre. We do condemn & value & assess the damages to said Frank to forty eight shillings [*illegible*].

And we think no other injury sustainable, & think no fish of passage nor navigation obstructed nor no mansion house, curtiledge, office, orchard nor garden nor health of the neighborhood will be injured thereby. In witness whereof we have hereunto set our hands & seals this 19th July 1806.

John Hendley	James Valendingham
Stephen Lay	Robert Boggs
James Whaley	Benjamin Grimes
William Scott	John Winn Jr.
John Gess	Benjamin Laughlin
Dennis Bradley	Leonard K. Bradley

Teste. Charles Carr S.F.C. The [*illegible*] named Thomas Frank came into court and made no opposition but consented that the mill might be erected, Thereupon the court do order that the said William Christian have leave to erect his dam agreeably to the report aforesaid.

Fayette County Order Book 1:403.

[28] *John Hendley vs. Edmund Bullock, executor of John S. Cockrill, deceased, Hamilton Jenkins and Thomas Franks*, Fayette County Circuit Court, Kentucky Land Trials, Record Book F:332. It is uncertain if George Sharp had a gristmill or some other type of mill. Sharp was the son-in-law of Robert Franks.

The heirs of Robert Franks sold John Hendley a tract of land near Athens, where Franks had operated a sawmill and hemp mill. In 1817, Hendley sued Franks' heirs to recover the mill seat, which the sellers claimed had been excluded from the deed.

[29] Photograph of the mill in Arthur Miller, *Geology of Kentucky* (Frankfort; 1919), p. 21. For an extensive investigation of the mill's origin, see Chris Amos and Nancy O'Malley, *Milling and Related Industry in the Boone Creek Drainage, Fayette and Clark Counties* (Lexington, 1991), p. 36, and Nancy O'Malley, Kentucky Archaeological Site Survey Form, Site No. 15 FA 213, Pettit Mill Complex, 1990, at the Kentucky Heritage Council.

[30] *Kentucky Gazette*, September 25, 1804.

[31] Fayette County Deed Book A:102. Deed dated 1803 for 45 acres. In 1805, Charles bought another contiguous tract of 20 ¾ acres. He purchased both of these tracts from Charles McPheters, paying 112 pounds 10 shillings for the first and $84 for the second. Fayette County Circuit Court Deed Book B:484.

The following year, 1806, Phillip Grimes died, and Charles inherited his father's homeplace—the 112 ½ acres on Baughman Fork.

[32] Fayette County Deed Book G:346. Lettice Winn's 60 acres were deeded to Grimes by Deputy Sheriff Charles Carr in November 1812. Charles paid 63 pounds for the tract.

[33] Fayette County Deed Book N:233. In the May 1815 deed of the 181-acre tract to Charles Grimes, Hendley reserved the rights to a one-acre mill seat "now claimed by George Sharp." Hendley had previously (1811) mortgaged the property to secure a loan for $1,300 from Charles Grimes, John Winn, and others. Fayette County Deed Book F:493.

John Hendley had a tavern near Athens and was married to Jemima Winn, daughter of George Winn. There are reports of Hendley buying flour and traveling between Athens and New Orleans, so we may infer that he was involved in the exporting business, possibly in association with Grimes.

After purchasing the Boone Station tract, Charles Grimes was involved in a lawsuit over it. His side came out the loser, and the tract had to be sold. The land brought four dollars an acre at a sheriff's auction. In some manner, however, Charles was able to get the property back, as his will devised the "Boons Station tract" to his daughter, Maria Monroe, wife of George Monroe. *David Castleman vs. estate of George E. Monroe, Charles Grimes, et al.* Fayette County Circuit Court, 1824; Fayette County Deed Book X:444; Fayette County Will Book N:198.

[34] Fayette County Deed Book S:460, U:365.

[35] In 1813, Grimes bought 94 acres in Fayette County on "the Waters of boons Creek" from Mordecai Gist for $846. Gist had obtained the tract from William Winn. Clark County Deed Book 9:294.

In 1818, Grimes bought 33 ½ acres from John Morgan. This tract was in the bend of Boone Creek on the Clark County side, just upstream from the mill. Clark County Deed Book 15:551.

In 1821, Grimes bought 28 acres on the waters of Boone Creek and Elk Lick Creek from Edward Stivers for $450. Fayette County Deed Book U:356.

In 1823, Grimes bought 21 acres on Boone Creek from the executors of George Walker's estate. This tract joined Charles Hazelrigg's property in Clark County and cornered on Hazelrigg's milldam. Fayette County Deed Book W:355.

[36] Grimes' bond to Graves, Fayette County Deed Book F:369; Graves' bond to Grimes found in *Levi Hart vs. James Vallandingham et al.*, Fayette County Circuit Court, Kentucky Land Trials, Record Book F:600. Three of the suits were *James Graves vs. Charles Grimes*, 1812, *James Graves*

and John Price vs. Charles Grimes, 1813, *Charles Grimes vs. James Graves*, 1820, Fayette County Circuit Court.

[37] *Charles Grimes vs. James Graves*, 1820, Fayette County Circuit Court. Graves answered that Grimes "did not pay the purchase money for the land as the plaintiff hath in declaring alledged."

Grimes was party to another suit over land, in which Levi Hart sought an order to make Grimes surrender his portion of 2,800 acres that Hart claimed on Boone Creek. *Levi Hart vs. Charles Grimes*, Fayette County Circuit Court, 1821. In 1821 and 1822, Hart entered similar suits against Henry Walker, George Monroe (Charles' son-in-law), Edward Stivers, David Devore, Samuel Berryman, and Jane Cotton. There is no evidence that any of these suits succeeded.

[38] These lots were obtained from Benjamin Harrison et al. in 1816 and from the trustees of Henry C. Clay in 1818. Clark County Deed Book 12:296, 14:403. Grimes paid $2,000 for the Winchester lots he obtained from Harrison.

[39] Clark County Deed Book 14:403. Clay, who had married Mary "Polly" Grimes in 1810, was indebted to James Langston of Winchester for $2,052. At the auction in January 1818, Charles Grimes bought the house and lot for the sum of $1,500.

[40] *Henry C. Clay vs. Charles Grimes*, Fayette County Circuit Court, 1815.

[41] Clark County Deed Book 12:298. Charles Grimes sold 179 acres to Benjamin Harrison of Clark County for 998 pounds by deed dated March 5, 1815.

In 1814, Charles Grimes bought from William Triplett's heirs a share in a large parcel of land bordering on the Kentucky River and the east side of Boone Creek. The land appears to have included much of Triplett's original patent of 1,845 acres. Grimes, John Wilkinson, and Henry Heronymous Jr. paid 5 shillings for the tract. A year later, Grimes sold Wilkinson his interest in the property for 5 shillings. Clark County Deed Book 10:86, 11:390.

In 1836, Charles Grimes sold a small parcel—17 acres—of the Stoner Creek property he had inherited from his father. Joseph Sewell bought the tract for $400. Clark County Deed Book 28:545.

[42] Arthur McFarlan, *Geology of Kentucky* (Lexington; 1943), p. 12. "Magnesian limestone" is an old term. The stone is now referred to as a "calcareous dolomite"—a dolomite (calcium magnesium carbonate) containing varying amounts of limestone (calcium carbonate).

[43] William Perrin, editor, *History of Fayette County, Kentucky* (Chicago; 1882), p. 33; Charles Richardson, *The Building Stones of Kentucky* (Frankfort; 1923), p. 125. The columns for the Old Capitol were erected in 1827. The Henry Clay monument was erected in 1857, the Daniel Boone monument in 1862.

Charles Grimes' son, Charles W., was evidently involved in quarrying operations in some fashion. An inventory of his personal property in 1872 included "1 lot of quarrying tools." Inventory in *William E. Wilkerson vs. C. W. Grimes et al.*, Fayette County Circuit Court, 1872.

[44] *Kentucky Statesman*, July 7, 1852.

[45] February 17, 1863, Fayette County Deed Book 38:142. There were a number of other quarries in the area, including one on Grimes Mill Road on the way up the hill from Boone Creek on the Clark County side. The latter may have been the scene of a tragic accident in 1938:

> A man believed to be Charlie Walker...   died in a Winchester hospital last night after the automobile in which he was riding plunged from Grimes Mill Road into an abandoned rock quarry.

Lexington Herald, January 7, 1938.

[46] The 1840 census listed only 12 men employed in quarrying in Fayette County. *Compendium of the Enumeration of the Inhabitants and Statistics of the United States as Obtained at the Department of State from the Returns of the Sixth Census, Volume 3* (Washington, D.C.; 1841), p. 263.

[47] Charles Grimes' estate inventory listed a total of 83 hogs. Fayette County Will Book N:306.

[48] *Charles Grimes vs. James Minter*, Clark County Circuit Court, 1828. Lease dated October 14, 1826; court order signed by William Hickman, May 1, 1828.

[49] Ibid. The attachment was served by William Sympson, deputy sheriff.

[50] Fayette County Will Book N:306. The business arrangement between Grimes and Minter is unknown. After erecting a dam and mill building, Charles would certainly have expected more of a return than $150 a year. He may have provided the raw materials and purchased the products at an agreed price.

Minter paid part of the rent he owed, and then on June 12, 1828 he mortgaged the furnishings of his factory to secure the balance of $155. The following is the full inventory of furnishings included in the mortgage:

one duble throstle unfinished but which I engage to finish with 42 spindles on each side, two new drawing fraims constructed on new planes, all the leather belts and bands I have about the factory, one slide laithe, one smith vice, two stocks for cutting screws, three iron shafts, one work bench and all other tools and apparatus I have for making machinery, one falling axe, my bridle and saddle, one cow and calf, and all my household and kitchen property.

Clark County Deed Book 23:196.

[51] Betty Kerr, "National Register of Historic Places Inventory, Nomination Form," 1980; Nancy O'Malley, Kentucky Archaeological Site Survey Form, Site No OSA-15 FA 209, Grimes flax mill, 1990, at the Kentucky Heritage Council; Iroquois Hunt Club's Horse and Hound Show Souvenir Program, Iroquois Hunt Club papers, Special Collections, M. I. King Library, University of Kentucky.

[52] *Charles Grimes vs. James Jenkins*, Fayette County Circuit Court, 1817.

[53] *James Graves vs. Charles Grimes*, Fayette County Circuit Court, 1819. About this time, Charles' brother, Benjamin Grimes, was also in the timber business in some fashion. In Henry Clay's papers, there is an itemized bill, dated July 8, 1817, from William Banton listing "Timber from Mr. Nettles to amount of $63.05 [and] from Benjamine Grymes [for] $79.16." A note added to the bill stated that "Mr. Banton is to endeavor to get Grimes's bill reduced, he charging four dollars instead of 3 ½ *for scantling*." Scantling is an old term for planking. James Hopkins, editor, *The Papers of Henry Clay, Volume 2* (Lexington; 1959), p. 363.

[54] *Lexington Herald*, March 18, 1928.

[55] John McCall had a distillery at his Oak Ridge Mills. *Kentucky Gazette*, August 7, 1810. Nearby on the waters of East Hickman Creek, Thomas Hart Jr. had a "merchant mill and distillery." *Kentucky Gazette*, January 24, 1809.

    Tench Coxe, *A Statement of the Arts and Manufactures of the United States of America for the Year 1810* (Philadelphia; 1810), p. 123. This valuable report lists the following manufacturers in Fayette County: 5 fulling mills, 1 flax seed oil mill, 1 paper mill, and 5 gunpowder mills. Unfortunately, gristmills were not enumerated. These Lexington figures were proudly announced in the local newspaper. *Kentucky Reporter*, February 23, 1811.

[56] *William Rout vs. Charles Grimes*, Fayette County Circuit Court, 1814.

[57] Deposition of John Bledsoe, 1816, *John Hendley vs. Edmund Bullock, executor of John S. Cockrill, deceased, Hamilton Jenkins and Thomas Franks*, Fayette County Circuit Court, Kentucky Land Trials, Record Book F:171.

[58] *Levi Hart vs. James Vallandingham et al.*, Fayette County Circuit Court, Kentucky Land Trials, Record Book G:14.

[59] *Levi Hart vs. Charles Grimes*, Fayette County Circuit Court, 1812.

[60] Ibid. Deposition of Polly Clay.

[61] Ibid. Court records reveal one other episode involving Cleveland. In 1824, Charles Grimes sued him for a debt of $75, which Cleveland had agreed to pay "for Rent of your place." The case was dismissed, most likely after Cleveland paid up. *Charles Grimes vs. Eli Cleveland*, Fayette County Circuit Court, 1825.

[62] Richard Spurr Sr. was in Kentucky in the fall of 1779, locating land in present-day Clark and Montgomery counties with Enoch Smith. In 1789, Spurr settled on Boggs Fork, on land he bought from Alexander Cleveland, Eli's brother. Spurr died in 1791, leaving a will in Fayette County. To Richard Jr. he left, among other things, 100 acres on Stoner Creek, his largest smooth gun, a watch, a featherbed, and two stills with "all the necessities belonging thereto." In 1811, Richard Jr. was unable to pay notes due to John Gess, James Vallandingham, and Nathaniel Winn totaling $739. To settle the notes, Spurr deeded over to the trio two slaves and "a certain roan horse." Richard Jr. was unmarried in 1815. James Spurr married Susanna Winn, sister of Jane Winn (Charles Grimes' wife). Deposition of Enoch Smith, Fayette County Circuit Court, Kentucky Land Trials, Record Book B:469; Fayette County Circuit Court Deed Book A:383; Fayette County Will Book A:336; Fayette County Deed Book E:427; Clark County Deed Book 11:396.

[63] *Richard Aubry et al. vs. Charles Grimes*, Fayette County Circuit Court, 1818.

[64] Ibid.

[65] Ibid.

[66] William Leavy, "A Memoir of Lexington and Its Vicinity," Nina Visscher, editor, *Register of the Kentucky Historical Society* (1943) 41:109.

[67] *Kentucky Gazette*, April 18, 1814.

[68] *Kentucky Gazette*, May 2, 1814. "Notice. The Co-partnership heretofore existing between Wm. Grimes, jr., and William H. Tegarden

under the firm of Wm. Grimes, jr. and Co. has been dissolved by mutual consent. The business of the firm devolves upon the subscriber. Wm. Grimes, Jr."

[69] *Kentucky Gazette*, November 13, 1815.

[70] *Kentucky Gazette*, June 26, 1815.

[71] July 18, 1816, deed of trust by William Grimes Jr., assigned "all the estate, real, personal & mixed, to which he the said [William] Grimes is entitled" to George Trotter Sr., Terence Cooney, William Ward Blair, and Percival Butler (all of Lexington), Fayette County Deed Book P:320. Grimes showed assets of $32,470, almost all of it in notes and accounts due.

[72] *John Hendley and John Scott vs. Charles Grimes and William Grimes Jr.*, 1817, *Bank of Kentucky vs. Charles Grimes and William Grimes Jr.*, 1817, *Neil and Hurley vs. Charles Grimes and William Grimes Jr.*, 1821, *Lewis Lay and Nicholas Thuron vs. Charles Grimes and William Grimes Jr.*, 1823, all in Fayette County Circuit Court.

[73] *Lewis Lay and Nicholas Thuron vs. Charles Grimes and William Grimes Jr.*, 1823, Fayette County Circuit Court. Lay and Thuron, the most vindictive creditors, sought to collect a $2,400 penalty bond against William and Charles Grimes, because William had agreed to stay "in the bounds of the Jail," and it was later found that "he did depart beyond... the bounds of the Jail." Lay's and Thuron's claim was not allowed, and they had to pay the defendants' costs.

One of the things that may have angered Lay and Thuron was an agreement William made with Henry C. Clay in January 1816. William made a deed of trust to Clay, assigning to him William's "dwelling house in which the said Grimes now keeps his store" as well as the "goods, wares and merchandise which he hath now on hands." This property was to be sold "for the benefit and relief" of Charles Grimes "in the event of failure in business of the said William Grimes Jr."—an "event" that Lay and Thuron perceived had already occurred. The deed must have appeared as a brazen attempt by William to sign away most of his assets and make Charles Grimes the beneficiary. Fayette County Deed Book N:402.

[74] *Kentucky Gazette*, February 5, 1816.

[75] William Jr. may have been the son of Charles Grimes, but the relationship is unproven. There were two William Grimeses at that time in Fayette County, one living near Athens and one living in Lexington. Both were young men, and it is supposed that William Jr. of Lexington was the younger of the two. If William Jr. was Charles' eldest son, it would

explain why Charles made such sizeable commitments to his business. It would also explain why William risked the ire of his creditors to make the deed of trust to Henry C. Clay for Charles' benefit. Clay was Charles' son-in-law. In the deed of trust, William gave up his rights "in the estate, real and personal, of his father." This could account for the omission of William in Charles' will. Another explanation for the omission may be that William died before Charles. From the *Kentucky Reporter*, August 23, 1820: "Died, in Madison County...William Grimes Jr." William is not named, however, in the Grimes family bible, which lists the children of Charles and Jane Grimes.

[76] Clay Lancaster, *Antebellum Houses of the Bluegrass* (Lexington; 1961), p. 18. The house, which is now owned by Charles and Gloria Martin, has been featured by *Life Magazine* (April 25, 1955); J. Winston Coleman, *Historic Kentucky* (Lexington; 1967), p. 53; and Richard DeCamp, *The Bluegrass of Kentucky* (Lexington; 1985), p. 33; and Bettye Lee Mastin, *Lexington Herald-Leader*, September 28, 1958.

[77] N. W. Embry, who lived there in 1898-99, wrote that the house dated from 1813, as "is evidenced by a stone bearing that date, now under the vines beneath the gable and chimney on the North side of the house." N. W. Embry to St. Louis Reinhardt, letter and notes, July 11, 1955, with copies to the Kentucky Historical Society and Filson Club.

[78] Bettye Lee Mastin reported on the "turned around house" and Clay Lancaster's evaluation that the lower two-story wing was the original house to which the main structure was added in 1813. *Lexington Herald-Leader*, September 28, 1958.

[79] Fayette County tax lists, 1835-1837.

[80] Charles was followed in death by his daughter, Maria Monroe, who died in 1844, and was buried in the Grimes cemetery. The cemetery was used between 1820 and 1856 and has thirteen marked graves. N. W. Embry to S. L. Reinhardt, letter and notes, July 11, 1955, Kentucky Historical Society.

[81] Fayette County Will Book N:198. Will signed May 15, 1837; probated October 1837. Other children named in the will include sons Owen and Sidney Grimes and daughters Polly Talbott (formerly Clay), Maria Monroe, Martha Jane Young, and Elizabeth Barkley. Some of them had moved out of Kentucky by 1837, as Charles stated in his will that he was "about to go *to the State of Missouri on a visit to see two of my children* and being desirous to dispose of my estate in the event of my death, do make ordain and publish this my last Will and testament."

[82] Fayette County Will Book N:306. The inventory of Charles Grimes' personal estate listed an appraisal value of $4,400.

Chapter 5. Middle Years, 1837-1887

[1] Julius MacCabe, *Directory of the City of Lexington and County of Fayette for 1838 and 1839* (Lexington; 1838). The directory listed 25 landowners living near Athens.

[2] Joel and Erasmus Grimes, sons of Charles W., served in John Hunt Morgan's cavalry, as did three other Grimeses from Lexington—John, J. H., and Thomas. State of Kentucky, *Report of the Adjutant General of the State of Kentucky, Confederate Kentucky Volunteers, War 1861-65, Volume 1* (Frankfort; 1915), pp. 698-702, 720.

Lewis Grimes was a Union veteran residing in Lexington in 1890. U.S. Census, Schedules of Civil War Union Veterans and Widows, 1890, Fayette County, Kentucky, p. 081.

[3] For a vivid account of the trials Kentucky faced during the war, see E. Merton Coulter, *The Civil War and Readjustment in Kentucky* (Chapel Hill, NC; 1926).

[4] James Prather, *City Directory of Lexington, Kentucky, 1890* (Lexington; 1890); U.S. Census, Schedules of Civil War Union Veterans and Widows, 1890, Fayette County, Kentucky, p. 068.

[5] U.S. Population Census, Slave Schedules, 1860, Clark County, p. 340, Fayette County, p. 408. The Thirteenth Amendment of the U.S. Constitution was ratified in December 1865.

[6] Thomas Clark, *Clark County, Kentucky, A History* (Winchester; 1996), p. 103. Clark was speaking of the period from 1792 to 1840.

[7] George Ranck, *History of Lexington, Kentucky* (Cincinnati; 1872), pp. 319, 365.

[8] U.S. Manufacturers Census, Fayette and Clark Counties, 1860; E. A. Hewitt, "Topographical Map of the Counties of Bourbon, Fayette, Clark, Jessamine and Woodford, Kentucky from Actual Surveys," 1861. Rogers Mill burned in the 1860s and was not reopened. No new mills would be built along the creek after the war.

Sarah Pettit acquired the mill from her father, James Pettit, who in turn had received the mill from his father, Nathaniel Pettit. Sarah married John Garrett in 1866, and in 1868 they sold the mill to Milton Christian. For a discussion of the complex title history of what is generally referred to as "Pettit's Mill," see Nancy O'Malley, Kentucky Archaeological Site Survey

Form, Site No. 15FA213, Pettit Mill Complex, 1990, at the Kentucky Heritage Council.

[9] E. A. Hewitt, "Topographical Map of the Counties of Bourbon, Fayette, Clark, Jessamine and Woodford, Kentucky from Actual Surveys," 1861.

[10] Carlo's name in county records was usually written as "Carlo," not "Carlow." In his father's will it was spelled "Carlow," but his signature always appeared as "Carlo." His name is written "Carlo" in the Grimes family bible, which gives his birth date as March 9, 1810. Copied in the *Louisville Courier Journal*, March 14, 1897.

[11] Carlo Grimes married Maria Louisa Talbott in Bourbon County on June 7, 1838, Reverend Dudley officiating. Bourbon County Marriage Register, Book 2:144.

[12] The deed from Benjamin Talbott, dated August 23, 1838, states that Carlo paid $25 an acre for the 110-acre tract. (Clark County Deed Book 28:581.) The deed gave Carlo's residence as Fayette County. The 1840 census listed him as a resident of Clark County, which suggests that he moved onto his new farm shortly after purchase.

Benjamin Talbott had purchased the farm from Hannah Hazelrigg in 1836. Hannah was the widow of Graham Hazelrigg and the heir of John Morgan, deceased. The tract was originally part of William Triplett's grant of 1,845 acres on Boone Creek. Old Virginia Grants, Volume 15:82; Clark County Deed Book 27:456.

[13] U.S. Population Census, Clark County, Kentucky, 1860, p. 028. Charles O. Grimes, age 22, was included in the household; he may have been a nephew. The same year, another Charles O. Grimes, age 15, was listed as the son of Charles W. Grimes.

Carlo's wife Louisa may have been the daughter of Daniel (1779-) and Elizabeth "Betsy" Talbott (1779-1825) of Bourbon County.

The 1840 census enumerated Carlo with a wife and no children. Children in the 1850-1870 population censuses included Jenny, Willis, Albert, Talitha, Charles P., John, Orren, and Clarence (Clarence was a female). Jenny was listed in 1850 as "Aria J.," age 8, and in 1860 as "Mary J.," age 18. The name on her marriage bond was "Ara Jane." Carlo is not found in the 1880 census.

Carlo's house is shown on an 1861 map of property owners. E. A. Hewitt, "Topographical Map of the Counties of Bourbon, Fayette, Clark, Jessamine and Woodford, Kentucky from Actual Surveys," 1861.

[14] The most telling evidence, perhaps, is the 1861 map, which indicates a gristmill on Boone Creek where Grimes Mill is located, one downstream at J. E. Rogers' and another upstream at Pettit's. On this map made just one

year after the census, no mills are shown on the Clark County side of the creek. E. A. Hewitt, "Topographical Map of the Counties of Bourbon, Fayette, Clark, Jessamine and Woodford, Kentucky from Actual Surveys," 1861.

[15] U.S. Manufacturers Census, Clark County, Kentucky, District No. 2, year ending June 1, 1860.

[16] Based on real estate values in the U.S. Population Census, Clark County, Kentucky, 1850.

[17] Madison County Marriage Records; U.S. Population Census, Fayette County, Kentucky, 1860, p. 470. Their children listed in the 1850-1870 population censuses were Erasmus D., Joel E., Charles O., Martha, Edwin R., Eucidius, William W., Talton E., Jesse E., Orlando, Ann W., Ruth D., and Jennie. Charles W. was born March 5, 1817. Grimes family bible, copied in the *Louisville Courier Journal*, March 14, 1897.

Mary Ann Embry's half-brother Jacob married Caroline Grimes in 1823 in Fayette County and her sister Ruth married Lewis Grimes in 1829 in Madison County. Caroline and Lewis were children of James Grimes, brother of the mill builder, Charles Grimes.

[18] Erasmus and Joel enlisted on September 10, 1862, just eleven days after the battle of Richmond. State of Kentucky, *Report of the Adjutant General of the State of Kentucky, Confederate Kentucky Volunteers, War 1861-65, Volume 1* (Frankfort; 1915), p. 720.

Elroy Stuart Cluke (1824-1863) was born in Clark County and raised on his grandfather James Stuart's farm. Cluke served in the Mexican War, and when General Bragg invaded Kentucky in 1862, Cluke raised a regiment for the confederacy from the Fayette-Clark-Bourbon county area. He participated in John Hunt Morgan's victory at Hartsville, Tennessee, and the Christmas Raid in 1862 and was captured during the Ohio raid in 1863. Cluke died in a Union prison at Johnson Island, Ohio, in December 1863. "Clark County Chronicles," in *Winchester Sun*, May 13, 1926; Kathryn Owen, *Civil War Days in Clark County* (Winchester; 1963), p. 50.

[19] Union losses under Major General William "Bull" Nelson were 206 killed, 844 wounded, and 4,303 missing. General Kirby Smith's losses were 98 killed, 492 wounded, and at least 10 missing. The victory sparked a wave of Confederate enlistment in central Kentucky. The battle opened General Braxton Bragg's massive invasion of Kentucky that ultimately failed with his defeat at Perryville in October 1862. D. Warren Lambert, *When the Ripe Pears Fell* (Richmond; 1995).

[20] *Lexington Herald*, March 18, 1928. The article incorrectly named the two as sons of Phillip; they were the eldest children of Charles W. Grimes,

Phillip's grandson. Erasmus Darwin Grimes (1840-1911) was listed in the 1860 census as a medical student and in 1870 as a physician. Joel Embry Grimes (1842-) was listed as a student in 1860 and a farmer in 1870. They were enumerated with their father's household both years.

[21] Bennett Young, *Confederate Wizards of the Saddle* (Nashville; 1914), p. 178. Also lending credence to the tradition is the fact that Cluke's forces can be placed within two miles of Grimes Mill on February 25, 1863:

> Clay's Ferry
> Rebels crossed here and at Boonesborough last night....
> I send you three prisoners...   all of Cluke's Kentucky regiment....   I will be in Mount Sterling or Paris at daylight.

Colonel Benjamin Runkle to General Q. A. Gillmore, *War of the Rebellion: A Compilation of the Official Records of the Union and Confederate Armies,* Volume 23, Part 2, p. 87. From Clays Ferry, Cluke's men could have taken Grimes Mill Road on their way to Mount Sterling.

[22] Charles W. Grimes bought two tracts adjoining his plantation in Fayette County from Jacob Embry, one in 1847 and one in 1853. He also bought a tract in Clark County in 1848 from Armistead Blackwell adjoining Carlo on the south side of Grimes Mill Road. Fayette County Deed Book 24:616, 29:151; Clark County Deed Book 34:18.

[23] Clark County Deed Book 44:520. The first tract was the 118 acres Charles W. had bought from Armistead Blackwell. The second tract was 33 ½ acres referred to as "the Morgan tract" that Charles Grimes had purchased from John Morgan and left to Charles W. and Carlo in his will. Clark County Deed Book 34:18, 15:551.

[24] Fayette County Deed Book 38:142.

[25] Fayette County Deed Book 38:112.

[26] *Lexington Herald*, March 18, 1928.

[27] Nancy O'Malley surveyed this site in 1990. She located and described the stone foundation of the distillery, about 30 feet by 40 feet, with two rooms, and a nearby spring. Kentucky Archaeological Site Survey Form, Site No. 15 FA 211, Grimes Distillery Site, at the Kentucky Heritage Council.

[28] Water warmer than 55 to 60 degrees would not efficiently condense alcohol vapor and could force a distiller to suspend operations. Gerald Carson, *The Social History of Bourbon* (Lexington; 1963), p. 43.

[29] U.S. Manufacturers Census, Fayette County, Kentucky, for the year ending June 1, 1870; "Distillers in the Seventh District of Kentucky," George Hodgman, *Kentucky State Directory, Travelers and Shippers' Guide for 1870-1871* (Louisville; 1870), p. 201. Poindexter & Pettit were Richard Poindexter & B. F. Pettit.

William Perrin reported that Grimes was a distiller in the Athens Precinct:

> C. W. Grimes built a small distillery on Boone's Creek in 1876, which is still [1882] in operation, with a capacity of 300 barrels per annum.

William Perrin, editor, *History of Fayette County, Kentucky* (Chicago; 1882), p. 212. Perrin may have intended 1866 or 1867 instead of 1876. It is unlikely that Grimes put any new distillery buildings or machinery into operation in 1876. By that time, he was in serious financial straits and had put all his properties into a trust to satisfy his creditors. A "typo" seems the most likely explanation for Perrin's date.

[30] In 1868, Henry Gibson billed Carlo Grimes $7.50 for "hauling Coal from River, 3 loads." Gibson billed another $7.50 for "hauling whiskey to town [Lexington]." *Henry Gibson vs. Albert D. Grimes and Carlo Grimes*, Fayette County Circuit Court, 1874.

[31] U.S. Manufacturers Census, Fayette County, District No. 1, year ending June 1, 1870. The concern reported revenue taxes equal to 60 cents per gallon. In 1868, the federal excise tax was 50 cents per gallon of 100 proof whiskey. Federal taxes were also assessed each year on stills, according to their capacity.

[32] U.S. Manufacturers Census, Fayette County, District No. 1, year ending June 1, 1870.

[33] U.S. Population Census, Fayette County, Kentucky, 1870, p. 10a. In 1850, William Lindsay, age 28, was listed with wife Mary, age 25, and their four children. They were living with Mary's widowed mother, Rachel Grimes, age 54, in Fayette County. James W. Lindsay's parents may have been the Thomas Lindsay, age 60, farmer, and his wife Elizabeth, age 57, listed in Clark County in 1850. They had previous mill experience as owners of Pettit's Mill. They sold the mill in 1832 to Nathaniel Pettit. U.S. Population Census, Fayette County and Clark County, 1850; Fayette County Deed Book 23:229.

In 1863, William Lindsay and his wife Mary sued Mary's brother, John F. Grimes, administrator of Rachel Grimes' estate, because of a disagreement over property in Rachel's estate settlement. Lindsay sued to have the accounts of John F. Grimes audited. John F. Grimes, age 45, farmer, was recorded as living in Lindsay's household in the 1870 census. *Lindsay vs. Grimes*, Fayette County Circuit Court, 1863.

[34] *John Gess and James Gess vs. E. R. Grimes and William Lindsay*, Fayette County Circuit Court, 1874. E. R. Grimes was Charles W.'s son Edwin. The Gess brothers sued to collect payment of $122, which they were owed by Grimes and Lindsay, mainly for threshing and hauling a large quantity of grain—992 bushels of wheat, 310 bushels of oats, and 260 bushels of barley.

[35] Fayette County Deed Book 46:227. Power of attorney dated March 23, 1869. Henry Gibson was a Clark County neighbor, shown on an 1877 map living about one-half mile south of Carlo. Gibson had prior connections to distilling. In the 1850 population census for Clark County, Henry Gibson, farmer, was enumerated with Granville Smitha, who operated a distillery on Boone Creek. Gibson died in 1878. D. G. Beers and J. Lanagan, *Atlas of Bourbon, Clark, Fayette, Jessamine and Woodford Counties, Kentucky* (Philadelphia; 1877); Clark County Settlement Book 22:532.

[36] Fayette County Deed Book 50:266.

[37] U.S. Population Census, Fayette County, 1870.

[38] Deed of trust from Charles W. Grimes to William E. Wilkerson, February 5, 1872, Fayette County Deed Book 50:266. The purpose of putting Charles W.'s property in his wife's name must have been to protect these assets from exposure to future creditors who might surface after the settlement of his affairs.

[39] E. Merton Coulter, *The Civil War and Readjustment in Kentucky* (Chapel Hill, NC; 1926), p. 145.

[40] *Lexington Observer and Reporter*, September 15, 1866.

[41] *Lexington Observer and Reporter*, February 12, 1868.

[42] *Lexington Observer and Reporter*, February 10, 1868. Aged bourbon was selling from $3.75 to $10 per gallon. The whiskey tax was assessed on alcohol content, the basis being a "proof gallon," i.e., one gallon of 100 proof whiskey. Gerald Carson, *The Social History of Bourbon* (Lexington; 1963), pp. 114-127.

Although the government broke up the Whiskey Ring, it continued to raise the excise tax on whiskey. The tax was up to $10.50 per gallon by 1951. Carson's book gives a good description of Kentucky's whiskey industry during these tumultuous times.

[43] Lowell Harrison and James Klotter, *A New History of Kentucky* (Lexington; 1997), p. 304.

[44] The manufacturers census of 1870 indicates that he owed revenue taxes totaling $8,400 for that year.

[45] Fayette County Deed Book 51:549. Grimes later claimed that he had paid the tax, and in 1877 he filed a lawsuit against A. H. Bowman in Fayette County Common Pleas Court.

[46] *Kentucky Statesman*, May 14, 1872. The notice was placed in the paper again on May 17, 21, and 30.

Deputy Collector R. P. Stoll was Richard P. Stoll (1851-1903) of Lexington. He started out in the Internal Revenue Department but soon became one of the giants of Kentucky's distillery industry. He was president of the Commonwealth Distilling Co. and afterward was engaged in the wholesale whiskey business as a principal in the firm of Stoll, Clay & Co. and then Stoll, Hamilton & Co. Stoll was also involved in banking, railroads, and the gas industry, and served several terms in the state legislature. J. S. Clarke Publishing Co., *History of Kentucky, Volume 3* (Louisville; 1927), p. 370.

[47] Fayette County Deed Book 51:549. The warehouse was "seized" by the revenue collector on May 10, 1872, "knocked down" at auction on June 1, 1872, and conveyed by deed to H. C. Clay of Bourbon County on June 12, 1873.

[48] Fayette County Deed Book 52:506, 507. Deed and Consent dated February 23, 1874. It is not clear how the distillery got transferred from H. C. Clay to Charles W. Grimes, as no indenture was recorded in the Fayette County deed books during that period. There may have been some other agreement between Clay and Grimes, which made Clay proprietor of the distillery. That this was the case is indicated by the power of attorney Clay signed on February 9, 1874:

> I, Henry C. Clay of the County of Bourbon and State of Kentucky do hereby constitute and appoint Charles Grimes of the County of Clark and State of Kentucky My true and lawful agent and attorney in fact to sign my name *as Distiller and Principal* to any Warehouse Bonds... that I may be required *as Distiller of the 7th District*, Kentucky, to execute.... (emphasis added)

Fayette County Deed Book 51:636. The "Charles Grimes of Clark County" was Carlo's 23-year-old son, Charles P. Grimes.

[49] *William E. Wilkerson vs. C. W. Grimes et al.*, Fayette County Circuit Court, 1872. The collection of papers included in this bundle is nearly two inches thick.

A Rockaway is a two-seat, four-wheel carriage named after the town in New Jersey where it was first made.

[50] *William E. Wilkerson vs. C. W. Grimes et al.*, Fayette County Circuit Court, 1872. The Report of Claims was dated February 1873; the sale of Charles' personal estate was in September 1872.

[51] Ibid. The court ordered a "public sale on the premises on the 20th of March 1873." The sale was to be advertised "for the period of two weeks in the *Lexington Observer & Reporter* newspaper." The paper ceased publication in March 1873.

The two parcels were sold on March 23, 1873, and the deeds were executed on May 26, 1876. For $3,757, Christian purchased 167 acres bounded by Boone Creek, Boggs Fork, McCalls Mill Road and Grimes Mill Road. Fayette County Deed Book 55:487, 584.

[52] Both depositions in *William E. Wilkerson vs. C. W. Grimes et al.*, Fayette County Circuit Court, 1872.

[53] *Lexington Press*, January 28, 1875.

[54] William Perrin, editor, *History of Fayette County, Kentucky* (Chicago; 1882), p. 492.

[55] D. G. Beers and J. Lanagan, *Atlas of Bourbon, Clark, Fayette, Jessamine and Woodford Counties, Kentucky* (Philadelphia; 1877). Grimes Mill is not shown on the map.

[56] Fayette County Deed Book 59:316. The court ordered sale was held on June 7, 1878, and the deed to Embry was dated May 29, 1879. The sellers were listed as "C. W. Grimes, Erasmus D. Grimes, Joel E. Grimes, Mattie Scott, Ben Scott, Edward R. Grimes, William W. Grimes, Jessie Grimes, Annie Grimes, Talton Grimes, Ruth B. Grimes, Orlando Grimes, and Jennie Grimes by H. M. Buford, Master Commissioner of the Fayette Circuit Court."

[57] Fayette County Deed Book 59:351. By deed dated June 6, 1879, Talton and Martha Embry sold Talton Grimes the house and 75-acre farm for $3,000.

On March 1, 1898, Talton Grimes, "an unmarried man," sold the house and farm to George Embry and Henry Embry of Jefferson County for $1,719, and the home was out of the Grimes family. The deed excluded one-fourth acre "enclosed by a stone fence and used as a grave yard." Grimes retained the right for his relations or "any of his friends of the Lindsay family" to continue to use the cemetery. Fayette County Deed Book 112:344.

In his letter and notes, July 11, 1955, N. W. Embry recited the chain of title of the home after it left his family. In 1900, George Embry sold his half interest in the property to his brother Henry Embry. In 1911, Henry Embry sold to D. D. Eldridge and others. Fayette County Deed Book 121:159, 162:262.

The property was transferred several times in 1911 and 1913 between members of the Eldridge family. In 1914, G. T. Eldridge and his wife Louise sold one-half interest in the property to Mrs. Katherine Mischler and Frank Mischler. Fayette County Deed Book, 163:596, 169:126, 176:278.

In 1919, G. T. Eldridge and his wife Louise, Mrs. Katherine Mischler "a widow," and Frank Mischler and his wife Mary conveyed the tract to Ollie and Julia Biddle of Bourbon County. In 1923, the Biddles sold to H. H. and Louise Givin, who in turn sold the property, still consisting of 75 acres, to S. L. and Virginia Reinhardt in 1954. The Reinhardts operated their business concerns here as the West Wind Farm. Fayette County Deed Book 191:290; 216:162; 559:152.

The Reinhardts subsequently sold the property to Robert Murphy, who sold to Mary Murphy, who in turn sold it to Charles and Gloria Martin.

[58] *Lexington Daily Press*, March 14, 1886.

[59] *Lexington Morning Transcript*, March 16, 1886.

[60] Transcribed as it appears in Fayette County Will Book 6:578. Signed May 12, 1881; probated in March 1886.

[61] It is not clear whether H. C. Clay was still a principal in the distillery. William W. Grimes may have been shielding the distillery from Clay's creditors, as Clay was experiencing financial problems at this time.

Grimes Mill was not listed in the 1880 manufacturers census and might have been assumed to be part of the distillery business. There were a number of other distilleries in the census which had associated mills that did not have a separate entry for the mill.

[62] U.S. Manufacturers Census, Fayette County, year ending May 31, 1880.

[63] N. W. Embry to S. L. Reinhardt, letter and notes, July 11, 1955, Kentucky Historical Society. N. W. Embry's father, Henry Embry, owned Grimes House from 1898 until 1911.

[64] Fayette County Deed Book 52:506.

[65] D. G. Beers and J. Lanagan, *Atlas of Bourbon, Clark, Fayette, Jessamine and Woodford Counties, Kentucky* (Philadelphia; 1877); *Western Citizen*, October 20, 1865.

Henry C. Clay, age 26, of Bourbon County married Ara Jane Grimes, age 22, of Clark County, at Carlo Grimes' residence on October 3, 1865,

Elder G. J. Smith officiating. Clay's occupation was listed as farmer. Clark County Marriage Bonds, Book 4A:39.

[66] Nancy O'Malley, *Stockading Up, A Study of Pioneer Stations in the Inner Bluegrass Region of Kentucky* (Lexington; 1987), pp. 52-55. Henry Clay's stone house in Bourbon County stands north of Escondida, between Green Creek and Kennedy Creek.

A detailed history of the Clay family may be found in Mary Rogers Clay, "The Genealogy of the Clays," *The Clay Family*, Filson Club Publication No. 14 (Louisville; 1899). The line of descent of H. C. Clay is given below. There are two Grimes marriages and one Winn marriage in the line.

Henry Clay M.D. (1736-1820) was born in Cumberland County, Virginia, and died in Bourbon County, Kentucky. He married Rachel Poval, and they had the following children: Elizabeth, John, Rebekah, Samuel, Rachel, Sally, Tabitha, Mary Ann, Henrietta, Mattie, Henry, and Letty.

Samuel Clay (1761-1810) served in the Revolutionary War and came to Kentucky after the war, settling on Green Creek in Bourbon County. He married Nancy Winn, daughter of George and Lettice Winn. Samuel and Nancy had the following children: Henry C., Letitia, Samuel, George, Littleberry, Richard, John, Thomas, Rachel, and William Green.

Henry C. Clay (1791-) married Mary "Polly" Grimes, the sister of Charles W. and Carlo, in Fayette County, September 10, 1810. They had the following children: Charles, Nancy, Samuel H., and Jane.

Samuel H. Clay (1813-1872) married Julia Kennedy and died in Bourbon County. He was buried in Paris Cemetery. The 1860 census for Bourbon County lists Samuel, age 40, farmer, wife Julia, age 45, son Washington K., age 22, farmer, son Henry C. Clay, age 21, farmer, son Charles G., age 15, daughter Mattie, age 10, son B. J., age 8, son Samuel G., age 6, son William D., age 3, and Mary Talbott, age 65 (Samuel's mother, who married Benjamin Talbott after her first husband died). Samuel was a wealthy farmer with real estate valued at $63,700 and personal estate at $35,500. Mary "Polly" Grimes Talbott died in 1866 at age 70. She is buried in the Paris Cemetery.

Henry C. Clay (1839-) was the son of Samuel H. Clay. He went by his two initials—H. C. Clay—no doubt, to distinguish himself from a number of other Henry Clays. He was called "Harry Clay." H. C. Clay was the grandson of Mary "Polly" Grimes, who was the sister of Carlo. H. C. Clay married Carlo's daughter Jennie, his second cousin.

[67] William Perrin, *History of Bourbon, Scott, Harrison and Nicholas Counties, Kentucky* (Chicago; 1882), pp. 453-454. "Colonel E[zekiel] F.

Clay was a student at Kentucky University when war was declared in 1861, and at once enlisted in the First Kentucky Mounted Riflemen, Confederate States Army, as a private. Later he organized a company, of which he was chosen Captain, with William Talbott, Harry Clay, and James T. Rogers, of 'New Forest,' as Lieutenants."

[68] Clark County Mortgage Book 2:126. Mortgage dated August 18, 1874. The loan was paid in full November 5, 1880.

[69] Clark County Deed Book 48:375. Carlo and Louisa conveyed 276 acres to Oscar and Charles Gillman for $6,145, taking $1,573 in cash and notes for the balance. Carlo and Louisa were residents of Fayette County when they signed the sale documents on October 28, 1880.

Carlo and Louisa retained Charles Stoll as their agent, giving him power of attorney to collect the payments due from the sale of their farm and to "do everything requisite and necessary to be done in and about the premises... as I might or could do if personally present." Clark County Deed Book 48:377.

[70] Fayette County Mortgage Book 8:45. Mortgage dated January 9, 1882.

[71] Fayette County Mortgage Book 9:123. Mortgage dated January 31, 1883; signed by Carlo and Louisa Grimes and H. C. and Jennie Clay.

Robert R. Stone was one of the original directors of the Fayette National Bank of Lexington, organized in 1870. He was prominent in local affairs in the late 1800s. William Perrin, editor, *History of Fayette County, Kentucky* (Chicago; 1882), pp. 122, 289, 413.

[72] James Prather, *City Directory of Lexington, 1890*. Carlo Grimes signed a note to Robert Stone on January 31, 1883. Stone filed a petition on December 20, 1884, stating that "Carlo Grimes has been dead for more than 12 months." Petition is in *C. W. Foushee vs. H. C. Clay et al.*, Fayette County Circuit Court, 1885.

[73] A copy of the policy was included in the papers for *C. W. Foushee vs. H. C. Clay et al.*, Fayette County Circuit Court, 1885. Insured by the German American Insurance Company of New York for one year beginning February 14, 1885. The cost of the policy was $35, and losses were payable to R. R. Stone.

This suit, which was filed on July 3, 1885, identified the owners of Grimes Mill as "H. C. Clay, Jennie Clay his wife, and the widow and heirs of Carlo Grimes, deceased." A paper filed with the suit stated that Carlo Grimes had died intestate and listed his children as Talitha Clay, wife of B. F. Clay of Scott County, Orin Grimes, Charles P. Grimes, John W. Grimes, Clarence C. Grimes, and Jennie Clay, wife of H. C. Clay.

[74] R. L. Polk & Co., *Kentucky State Gazetteer and Business Directory, 1881-82.* Stoll, Clay & Co. purchased "Distillery No. 12" at Sandersville in 1880. William Perrin, editor, *History of Fayette County, Kentucky* (Chicago; 1882), p. 210.

Stoll, Clay & Co. closed in 1885, with the Stolls buying all of Clay's assets in the company. The public sale of his assets was announced in the newspaper. *Lexington Daily Press,* August 11, 1885. Clay subsequently announced he would contest the sale. *Lexington Morning Transcript,* August 12, 1885.

H. C. Clay was listed as a resident of Lexington in 1881. His home was on the north side of High Street between Limestone and Rose. C. S. Williams, *Lexington Directory, City Guide, and Business Mirror, 1881.*

[75] *C. W. Foushee, assignee of H. C. Clay vs. H. C. Clay, Jennie Clay his wife, R. R. Stone, et al.,* Fayette County Circuit Court, 1885.

[76] Fayette County Deed Book 74:53. The court ruled for Foushee in May 1885 and ordered the property sold. The public auction was held on August 10, 1885. Robert Stone, the purchaser, received promissory notes for $1,396, against which he held a lien on the property. Charles P. Grimes gave Stone a note for $1,000, due in August 1886, and Hector Lewis gave Stone a note for $396, due in January 1886, both at 8 percent.

Charles P. Grimes was listed in Carlo's household in the 1870 census as twenty years old and "works at home." Charles P. and Mary were listed in the 1880 census for Clark County. Their household included a son, Clay, age 5 months; a brother, Orren Grimes, age 24; and a sister, Mariah Hampton, age 30. Charles P. Grimes married Mary "Mollie" Lewis, so Hector Lewis may have been his brother-in-law.

[77] *Robert R. Stone vs. Mary M. Grimes, C. P. Grimes her husband, and Hector Lewis,* Fayette County Circuit Court, 1886.

[78] Fayette County Deed Book 78:47. The court ruled in February 1887, and the sale was held on March 14, 1887. Stone paid $1,100 for the property, which was deeded to him on June 8, 1887.

Chapter 6. Late Years, 1887-1928

[1] R. L. Polk and Co., *Kentucky State Gazetteer and Business Directory, 1887-88.* The 1879 gazetteer had reported Athens with a population of 287 and 19 businesses.

[2] *Kentucky Leader,* June 6, 1888; R. L. Polk and Co., *Kentucky State Gazetteer and Business Directory,* 1896; Lexington Advertising Co., *Rural Directory of Fayette,* 1912; Kentucky Directory Co., *Rural Directory of Fayette County,* 1926.

[3] This wheel was manufactured by the Fitz Water Wheel Co., which began making steel wheels in 1852. Thus, the steel wheel at Grimes Mill could have been installed by Charles W. and Carlo (before 1873), by Carlo and H. C. Clay (1873-1885), or by one of the owners in the late years.

[4] Fayette County Deed Book 83:325. Deed dated March 11, 1889.

[5] W. R. Wallis, "Map of Fayette County, Kentucky," 1891. A subsequent map in 1904 lists "J. McCuddy" as owner of the house directly across the road from the mill. J. P. Mullin and J. M. Corbin, "Map of Fayette County, Kentucky," 1904.

The rural directory for Fayette County in 1912 does not list any McCuddys living near Grimes Mill or in the county. The residents on Grimes Mill Pike at that time were Thomas and Lura Brumagen, D. D. and Annie Eldridge (residents of the Grimes House), George and Belle Fishback, Lucian Fishback, T. J. and Emma Hart, J. M. Hart, Reuben Maddux, D. D. and Martha Rankin, Martin Stone, and Sylvester and Millie Stone. Lexington Advertising Co., *Rural Directory of Fayette County,* 1912.

[6] Fayette County Deed Book 166:90. Deed dated August 8, 1912. Martha McCuddy was listed in the 1914 Lexington directory as widow of O'Connell "Mack" McCuddy, residence at 316 South Ashland Avenue; in the 1916 directory, she was living with her son Lindsay McCuddy on Oldham Avenue. She died in Lexington on May 17, 1925, at age 75, and was buried in Lexington Cemetery. R. L. Polk and Co., *Lexington City Directory,* 1914-15, 1916-17; *Lexington Herald,* May 18, 1925.

Martha's son, Charles McCuddy (1869-1938) maintained the family connection to milling. He spent many years working for the Lexington Roller Mills. *Lexington Herald,* March 18, 1938.

[7] R. L. Polk and Co., *Lexington City Directory,* 1906-07, 1914-15.

[8] Deeds dated August 30, 1913, and December 4, 1914, respectively. Fayette County Deed Book 171:217, 218; 176:404; R. L. Polk and Co., *Lexington City Directory,* 1902-03, 1912, 1914-15.

From 1916 until 1919, the Gaitskills lived on East Maxwell Street. Nannie died in Lexington on April 23, 1919, at the age of 69. Charles does not appear in later city directories. *Lexington Herald,* April 20, 1919.

[9] Fayette County Deed Book 38:142.

[10] Fayette County Deed Book 179:587. Deed dated November 29, 1915. The description of the Grimes Mill tract used in this deed has been copied in all subsequent deeds transferring the property.

[11] Fayette County Deed Book 179:587.

[12] R. L. Polk and Co., *Lexington City Directory*, 1914-15, 1916-17, 1921. Allie Webb was a widow when she died in Lexington in 1974. *Lexington Herald*, January 29, 1974.

[13] Fayette County Deed Book 183:42. Deed dated September 23, 1916.

[14] R. L. Polk and Co., *Lexington City Directory*, 1919, 1921, 1923, 1925, 1927. Charles' wife, Fannie Smitha, may have been descended from the Smitha family of Clark County. Granville Smitha operated a distillery on Boone Creek around 1870. Fannie died in 1921. Charles Lindsay died of pneumonia on January 26, 1936, at the age of 79 and was buried in the family plot in Lexington Cemetery. *Lexington Leader*, January 27, 1936.

[15] Fayette County Deed Book 205:383; 210:267. Deeds dated January 11, 1921, and March 25, 1922, respectively.

[16] Lexington Advertising Co.*, Rural Directory of Fayette County*, 1912; R. L. Polk and Co., *Lexington City Directory*, 1925, 1927.

[17] Fayette County Deed Book 221:627, 628. Deeds dated November 20, 1923. The Bowens sold lot numbers 440 and 441 in the Wickliffe Land Company's "Addition to the City of Lexington."

[18] U.S. Population Census, Powell County, Kentucky, 1880; R. L. Polk and Co., *Lexington City Directory*, 1912, 1923. A brief notice recalling his service in Powell County appeared in *the Clay City Times*, April 17, 1902:

> Deputy Sheriff J. M. Kennon and Jailer Y. C. Bowen passed through here Saturday with two fellows by the names of Ghent and Farthing, suspected of the Irvine post office robbery. They took them over to Irvine and left them in custody of Estill Authorities.

Another biographical bit comes from a *Clay City Times* article on May 3, 1906, which stated that

> Y. C. Bowen has purchased a new brick machine and will manufacture the brick for the new [bank] building near the site [in Stanton].

Additional information about Y. C. Bowen is provided in his obituary in the *Clay City Times*, January 19, 1939:

> York C. Bowen, 76, died Friday, January 6, at the home of his daughter, Mrs. Frank Mischler, in Lexington, following a long illness. He was born at Filson, this county, the son of William and Mary Reynolds Bowen. He was a member of the Christian church, of the Masonic Order, and the Odd

Fellows lodge.   Funeral Saturday afternoon by the Rev.
Archer Gray; burial in the Lexington cemetery.   Surviving
are his wife, Mrs. Anne Guthrie Bowen.... Mr. Bowen was
a resident of Powell county until 1912, when he moved to
Fayette county.   He served one term as jailer of this county
and had many friends here.

[19] In 1914, Frank and Katherine Mischler bought one-half interest in the
Grimes House, which they sold in 1919 to Ollie and Julia Biddle. (Fayette
County Deed Book 176:278, 191:290.) This Grimes connection occurred
at a time prior to York Bowen owning the mill. Frank Mischler Jr. died on
July 3, 1964, at the age of 74. *Lexington Herald*, July 4, 1964.

[20] *Clay City Times*, May 26, 1927.

[21] Ronald Deutsch, *New Nuts Among the Berries* (Palo Alto, CA; 1977), p.
153.

Chapter 7. Iroquois Hunt Club

[1] Iroquois Hunt Club papers, Special Collections, M. I. King Library,
University of Kentucky.   The papers include newspaper clippings,
correspondence, and other materials related to the Hunt Club collected by
Frances Lathrop Smith Dugan Shine (1903-1977).

The reported "founding date" bounced around a bit. The souvenir
program for the Horse and Hound Show in May 1928 stated "Iroquois
Hunt. Established in 1883 by the late Gen. Roger D. Williams." The
program from the Second Annual Horse and Hound Show in June 1929
stated "Iroquois Hunt. Established in 1880 by the late Gen. Roger D.
Williams."

Roger Williams was a well-known figure in the Bluegrass region and
beyond. From a brief biography published in the 1898 edition of *Land and
Water*:

Colonel Roger D. Williams of Lexington, Ky., is a typical
gentleman sportsman and perhaps deserves to be mentioned
in connection with Mr. [Theodore] Roosevelt, as he is to
raise at the request of Mr. R. a company of riders for the
lieutenant colonel's regiment from the troopers of the
Bluegrass region of Kentucky.   Unquestionably, his
company will be the best-mounted one in the regiment, for it
will be difficult to beat the Kentucky thoroughbreds these
hundred men will have. Mr. Williams is 42 years old, and
his straight six feet of height and 200 pounds of weight, his

litheness of limb, and his superb health make him physically an ideal leader for such a troop. He is an expert horseman and cross-country rider, is vice president and organizer of the National Fox Hunters Association, and serves as master of the hounds at their annual meets.

Quoted in the *Lexington Herald*, January 11, 1942.

[2] The founding date of 1880 and source of the Iroquois name were confirmed by the research of Hunt Club secretary, John Gourlay. He confirmed that Iroquois won the English Derby in 1881. The apparent inconsistency is explained by the fact that Iroquois "had a brilliant record in this country in 1880 and was the outstanding horse of the year." Letter from John Gourlay to Henry Vaughn, January 8, 1929, collection of Jerry Miller, Lexington.

[3] W. Fauntleroy Pursley's handbook for members, *Iroquois Hunt* (Lexington; 1955).

[4] *Lexington Herald*, January 11, 1942.

[5] Undated telegram from Frances Smith and Billy McDowell to Arnold Hanger, Iroquois Hunt Club papers, Special Collections, M. I. King Library, University of Kentucky.

Hunting terms were defined in Fauntleroy Pursley's handbook for members. The "field" is the riders, considered collectively, who follow the hounds in a hunt. "Giving tongue" is the sound a hound makes when working the line of the quarry. "Go to ground" refers to the fox going into his burrow or hole.

[6] Fayette County Deed Book 248:497. Deed dated March 21, 1928.

[7] Iroquois Hunt Club papers, Special Collections, M. I. King Library, University of Kentucky. Letter dated March 24, 1928.

[8] Ibid. John Pursley had previous involvement with the mill. The "Pursley Brothers" at some point acquired Charles Lindsay's notes on the property. The Pursley Brothers held the lien until John Pursley attested in November 1923 that the notes had been paid in full. Fayette County Deed Book 210:267.

[9] *Lexington Herald*, March 18, 1928.

[10] A number of improvements were described in a 1931 article in *Chase Magazine*:

Was at the Iroquois Hunt Kennels at Grimes Mill recently. They have certainly worked wonders on this place. The hill that was so hard to pull, even in low, has been changed so

> that it makes it very easy to go up now. That is
> Improvement No. 1. Improvement No. 2: The mill has been
> done over from A to Z. It is most livable and attractive.
> Think the chairman of this committee was Mrs. Kendall
> McDowell. She is to be congratulated. Improvement No. 3:
> The kennels have been rebuilt.... Improvement No. 4: A
> beautiful stable [was built] that will hold about twenty
> horses.

It is possible that Improvement No. 2 included removal of the mill-related machinery.

[11] N. W. Embry to S. L. Reinhardt, letter and notes, July 11, 1955, Kentucky Historical Society.

[12] *Lexington Herald-Leader*, November 4, 1962. Described in greater detail in the *Lexington Herald*, October 6, 1963.

[13] Dozens of such articles may be found in the Iroquois Hunt Club papers, Special Collections, M. I. King Library, University of Kentucky.

[14] *Lexington Herald-Leader*, November 4, 1962.

[15] *Lexington Herald-Leader*, October 29, 2000.

Epilogue

[1] Some excellent work has been done in Kentucky but coverage of the subject remains limited. See "Further Reading." One of the largest millstone collections in the U.S. may be viewed at Levi Jackson State Park in Laurel County, Kentucky. Larry Meadows and the members of the Red River Historical Society have assembled and documented an impressive collection of millstones and milling equipment at the museum in Clay City. In addition, they have conducted a number of field investigations of mill sites in central Kentucky, including Abbott's Mill on Lulbegrud Creek and Wade's Mill on Stoner Creek. For reports, see *Lexington Herald-Leader*, March 6, 2000, and December 27, 2000, and *Winchester Sun*, April 29, 2000.

Appendix C: Grimes Family History

[1] Kathrine Gottschalk and Anne Reddy, *Grimes Family* (n.p.; 1947); Elsie Dixon, *Our Ancestry* (North Sacramento, CA; 1950); Elizabeth Hawthorne and Nina Grimes, *The Grimes Family* (n.p.; 1974); Pearson Grimes, family history attached to a letter written to Fauntleroy Pursley, 1976; and other

unpublished genealogies provided by Diana McGinness, Russell Thompson, and Neil Smith.

[2] Pearson Grimes gave this date of birth in Sheffield, England, citing "a Bible record." Family history attached to a letter written to Fauntleroy Pursley, 1976. Hawthorne and Grimes in *The Grimes Family* gave the date of birth as 1693 in Maryland.

[3] From Nicholas Grimes' will. Loudoun County (Virginia) Will Book A:144.

[4] Nicholas Grimes Jr. died in 1789, reportedly on a trip out to Kentucky. His wife Jane and several of his children (William G., Sylvester, Edward, and Nicholas) resided in Bourbon County. *Benjamin Grimes vs. Sylvester Grimes, executor of William G. Grimes*, Bourbon County Circuit Court, 1815.

[5] From Phillip Grimes' will. Fayette County Will Book B:53. John, Stephen, and Phillip Jr. died before the will was written in 1805.

[6] From Charles Grimes' will and Grimes family bible. Fayette County Will Book N:198; bible records copied from the *Louisville Courier Journal*, March 14, 1897.

[7] Children from Charles Grimes' will. Fayette County Will Book N:198.

[8] From U.S. Population Census, Clark County, Kentucky, 1850, 1860, 1870.

[9] From U.S. Population Census, Fayette County, Kentucky, 1850, 1860, 1870.

[10] Mary Rogers Clay, "The Genealogy of the Clays," *The Clay Family*, Filson Club Publication No. 14 (Louisville; 1899). Ernest Clay died young, unmarried.

[11] From U.S. Population Census, Bourbon County, Kentucky, 1860; Mary Rogers Clay, "The Genealogy of the Clays," *The Clay Family*, Filson Club Publication No. 14 (Louisville; 1899).

[12] From U.S. Population Census, Fayette County, Kentucky, 1850, 1870.

Appendix E: Peter Paul, Stonecutter

[1] *Lexington Herald*, February 21, 1929.

[2] *Lexington Herald*, March 18, 1828.

[3] Peter Paul was not on the tax rolls for Fayette County in 1800 or 1801. In 1802, he appeared on the rolls with two tithables (white-males over 21

years of age) and no property. The following year the rolls listed "Peter Paul & Son," two tithables and one town lot valued at $100.

    John Gourlay, who wrote a historical sketch of Grimes Mill, stated that Peter Paul came out from Philadelphia. Quoted in *Lexington Herald*, January 11, 1942.

[4] *Kentucky Gazette*, May 7, 1802.

[5] Joseph Charless' 1806 Lexington Directory copied in Charles Staples, *The History of Pioneer Lexington*, 1779-1806 (Lexington; 1939), p. 252.

[6] Carolyn Murray-Wooley and Karl Raitz, in *Rock Fences of the Bluegrass* (Lexington; 1992), p. 152, did not include "stone cutters" in their list of stonemasons. Their rationale being that

> Stone cutters, stone sawyers, stone setters, marble cutters, and marble workers often lived in the household or neighborhood of a marble agent, tombstone shopkeeper, or manufacturer of monuments. Stone cutters, therefore, were probably tombstone carvers, not fence builders.

By logical extension, they probably were not mill builders either.

[7] Ibid., p. 104. The authors stated that Paul was an Ulster-Scot (i.e., "Scotch-Irish"), and that his crew may have consisted of Scotch-Irish laborers rather than Irish Catholics.

[8] A copy of this bond made in 1810 is found in *Levi Hart vs. James Vallandingham et al.*, Fayette County Circuit Court, Kentucky Land Trials, Record Book F:600.

[9] Fayette County District Court Deed Book D:322. Lot No. 34 measured 66 feet along Market and was 98 feet deep. Hugh McDermid sold the lot to Catherine Wood for 20 pounds in 1799. Fayette County Circuit Court Deed Book A:464.

[10] Fayette County Order Book 1:122.

[11] William Leavy, "A Memoir of Lexington and Its Vicinity," Nina Visscher, editor, *Register of the Kentucky Historical Society* (1943) 41:330. Leavy was describing the residents during the period from 1807 to about 1810.

[12] J. Winston Coleman, *Lexington's Second City Directory, Published by William Worsley and Thomas Smith for the Year 1818* (Lexington; 1953).

[13] *Kentucky Gazette*, March 20, 1810. The "Kentucky Farmer" followed many earlier assaults on foreigners. His letter is quoted at length here to show the depth of feelings being expressed at that time.

I have no notion at all that we are to be taught and instructed
by foreigners; that such fellows as Essex should pretend to
take the lead in bookbinding, Paul in stone cutting, Beck to
teach painting, Stedman or Wilkinson lock and white smith's
work; that McBean or Brand or Miller or Weir or Smith or
Monk should pretend to superintend or be partners in hemp
or weaving manufactories, Marsh make machinery,
Skidmore (the little iron man) to controul on the Knobs; that
Todd or Jones or Bordman or Wrigglesworth or Lees or
Brown or Walker or Williamson and Williams should
presume to establish or assist in cotton or woollen
manufactories, Uslier to build a theatre and make umbrellas,
or an Instone, a McAllister or a Bishop appear amongst the
benefactors of this state, a Frazer to regulate our watches and
time pieces, a Whitney and Wilson and Challen to furnish
our houses, Smith as a millwright, and Shaw to dig wells.
All those improvements ought to be left to our own native
born citizens—and such presumptuous "cut throats" have
received their desserts.

[14] Fayette County Order Book 2:347. Paul made his sills in 1811 for
Lexington's third courthouse, a three-story brick edifice erected in 1806. J.
Winston Coleman, *The Court-Houses of Lexington* (Lexington; 1937), p.
15.

[15] *Peter Paul vs. Pew and Chamberlin* and *Peter Paul vs. Henry Purviance,*
Fayette County Circuit Court, 1810.

[16] Fayette County Deed Book C:313, D:78. Each lot measured 32 feet by
104 feet. The adjoining property was owned by Dr. Elisha Warfield and
Henry Purviance.

The Pauls had many dealings with Henry Clay. Their names appear
frequently in his papers between 1808 and 1816. James Hopkins, editor,
The Papers of Henry Clay, Volumes 1 and 2 (Lexington; 1959).

[17] Fayette County Deed Book F:534. Peter Paul Jr. bought the lot in 1812,
paying $575 to the executors of Thomas Hart Jr.

According to Clay Lancaster, Paul's house at 220 Market Street was a
two-story, three-bay brick house with pegged window frames and a Greek
Revival recessed doorway. Peter Paul Jr. reportedly sold the house to Mrs.
Jane Richey in 1818. Clay Lancaster, *Vestiges of the Venerable City*
(Lexington; 1978), p. 229.

[18] *Kentucky Reporter*, May 1, 1816, and April 8, 1818.

[19] The Madison Hemp and Flax Spinning Company was on Silver Creek in Madison Creek.

[20] Fayette County Will Book E:544.   Will dated October 18, 1815; probated November 1822. After his wife's death, daughter and son were to equally divide the Market Street lot and the Pennsylvania property.   Son Peter was to get the lot on Upper Street "near the stray pen" and the shares of Madison stock.   Daughter Sarah was to get all of the "household and kitchen furniture."

Peter Paul Jr. carried on the stone trade in Lexington for a number of years.   In the 1840s, he cut and lettered a set of tombstones for the family cemetery at Howard's Grove, Robert Wickliffe's plantation that was located between Paris Pike and Bryan Station Road.   He charged $97.45 for four stones.   Wickliffe-Preston Papers, Special Collections, M. I. King Library, University of Kentucky.

Index